The Price

of

Being Thin

The Price
of
Being Thin

a personal chronicle of
my journey
by

Valerie Evans Goddard

This book is a work of fiction. Names, characters, places and incidents are either product of the author's imagination or are used fictitiously. Any resemblance to actual events, locales, persona, living or dead, is entirely coincidental.

THE PRICE OF BEING THIN

Cover Art and Design by Johnny Barlow
Interior Layout and Design by CH Creations

Published December 2008

CYPRESS

Cypress is an imprint of RoseHeart Publishing
www.roseheartbooks.com

ISBN 10: 0-9822337-0-1
ISBN 13: 978-0-9822337-0-2

Printed in the United States of America

FOREWORD

The first question every author faces without exception begins "give a short synopsis of your book." This book is about pain and a steadfast, stubborn will to survive. "The Price of Being Thin" is my story detailing a lifetime of obesity, the constant struggle of dieting, loneliness at being an outcast in a slender world, and finally the decision to do something radical about it then contending with the fall-out from that decision. The saying, "be careful what you wish for" applies here.

As John Donne, in the seventeenth century once wrote, "no man is an island," likewise all those who love me share this story. Obesity has been scientifically confirmed as genetic and based on that premise a good many of my family walk this path with me. "The Price of Being Thin" reveals the anguish of living with the decisions I have made then leading on to the ultimate cost of that momentous decision. I am eternally grateful for the love and support I have been so fortunate to have. It is those bonds that have given me a reason to wake up every morning and continue to feed my steadfast will to survive another day.

I refuse to generalize. This book concerns only my experiences and my opinions of gastric by-pass surgery. In saying that, I realize there are many thousands of men and women who have experienced extreme complications of this surgery. However, to avoid any liability, I will not specifically mention anyone. To avoid any defamation problems I will only loosely identify the doctors and hospitals that have and continue to treat me or further to include the names of anyone else who is involved. This book is not a medical journal. These experiences are very personal. I am not a doctor, I am merely a patient who knows her body or who once did before gastric by-pass surgery changed everything.

Is that enough of a disclaimer? I certainly hope so. In comparison, I will from time to time refer to my sister's gastric by-pass surgery (with her permission), which was performed at a different hospital and under the care of a very different surgeon. My sister's surgery was "successful" and yet there are still problems that she continues to face everyday. I do not wish to hurt or offend anyone with the writing of this story. I have fought the writing of this book for longer than anyone might imagine. Ultimately, I am a writer and this story, my story, is one that I must tell.

Every time I see a celebrity take the public forum to speak about the wonders of gastric by-pass surgery, I feel so many things. These celebrities are setting an example, whether they mean to or not. I feel happy for anyone who has found some respite from their pain, however, I know what the consequences can be to this very serious surgery. I feel saddened their more often than not a rosy picture often influences others to rush into this surgery without knowing, really knowing, there are extreme complications for which few people can ever be prepared.

Slowly, doctors, medical personnel, scientists and researchers are beginning to discover the pitfalls of certain bariatric procedures. The lasting complications, physically and mentally, are becoming all too frequent and devastating. I will be forever grateful for the care so many medical personnel, doctors, and nurses have given me who have miraculously saved my life. Yet there are others, who should never be allowed loose on the unsuspecting public as well as given a license to administer medical care.

So what is the purpose of this book? First, most importantly to me, this work is my personal therapy. This book is a vehicle to share the struggle that I will continue to face every day for the remainder of my life. Further, I want to say that this surgery has changed my life, both negatively and positively. Unfortunately, for me, the bad has by far outweighed the good. On a final note, I am sorry to say the proceeds from this work will cover a small portion of my medical expenses; they are extensive and growing daily.

So, what is "The Price of Being Thin?" God, I just pray it is not my life.

ACKNOWLEDGEMENTS

Primarily my husband deserves every accolade possible. He is, simply put, the reason that I am still alive today. It is only through his love and commitment that I have managed to survive this ordeal. I can never thank him enough; his love has always been unconditional, his only desire being that I am healthy and happy. Secondly, one of my deepest regrets is the pain that our children have suffered through years of constant worry for me. My children are the light of my life. I live for them, through them.

Our extended families have spent countless hours at my bedside in the various hospitals, constantly calling for updates, and lifting me up in prayer. Each of them has been wonderful during our time of need. Friends have stood beside us, sharing this burden of pain we have endured. Dear family and friends, a simple thanks along with all the love in my heart is all that I have to give in exchange for your sleepless nights and troubled days while preparing for the worst and hoping for the best.

My heart fills with love for a wonderful friend who connected me with my university doctor who finally turned my life around. This friend, in her concern for me, saved my life. Special thanks are due to my university doctor, his staff and the bevy of interns who slowly brought me back from the brink of certain death. Local doctors, specialists, and wonderful nurses continue to contribute to my sometimes-daily struggle to live. The nurses who have come into our home have been true angels of mercy. Fate delivered me to the amazing doctors who care for me now. Additionally, their exceptional staffs make every visit painless, at least administratively. With gentle medical care and guidance, I am living moment to moment in this constant battle to survive.

Dedication

To my sister, Cindy Evans Felkins,
who is beautiful in every possible way.
I am so very proud of you and love you dearly.

Chapter One

~ *WHEN I WAS YOUNG* ~

"Chubby as a chipmunk." Doesn't that sound cute? I was a chubby baby as a toddler, I had big rosy cheeks and a huge drool-soaked grin. I never felt any different from my playmates. I was simply a happy, spoiled baby girl.

By kindergarten, a few things had changed. I was the kid who couldn't quite keep up with the other boisterous pre-schoolers in my class at recess when we played games. When first grade rolled around, I quickly became aware of the pecking order. Isn't it funny how even in a pack of small children, cliques are born? Learning my place was not a pleasant discovery, so I pretended to ignore the painful slights while my self-esteem plummeted to the depths of utter despair.

Classically, I was the fat kid picked last for team games on the schoolyard. I donned a protective armor to shield my sensitive feelings by acting bossy and self-important. I thought my peers would gravitate toward me if I took a leadership roll (of course, in my grade school mind, the concept was much more simplistic), still, no one in my class wanted to be my friend. I often arrived home in tears with taunts of "fatty-fatty" ringing in my ears, my delicate ego crushed. Mother gently soothed me with a treat. Imagine my big green eyes bright with tears, peering from beneath pageboy bangs and telling my mother "no one will play with me." "Have another cookie" was the loving response that lifted my spirits and eased my bruised feelings. Food quieted my emotional hunger, however, my sensitive composure was never completely sated.

As the early grades progressed, Mother thought she could keep me at a manageable weight by criticizing and cajoling. Honestly, Mama did what she thought was best for me. Yet the criticism only added weight to my ever expanding physique and deflated my steadily declining self-esteem. My mother loved me very, very much. She just had no idea how to cope with my weight problem. Times were different when she grew up; people were generally more accepting of one another. In her day, children were taught, "if you can't say something nice, say nothing at all" and if you did not obey the strict mantra, an Ivory soap bar wasn't exactly a tasty snack.

Honestly, I don't remember what I weighed during my adolescent years. I remember my school jeans came from Sears boy's "husky" section. I was so embarrassed because the pants always had the size emblazoned on an ugly brown waist band tag for everyone to see my shame. The word "HUSKY" appeared in all caps as obvious as a blinking neon sign. As for the remainder of my clothing, Mother made most of them. She was an excellent seamstress.

Our family has always been a crowd of "big-boned people"; even my mother (who was generally only fifteen to twenty pounds overweight), managed to chunk up a bit from time to time. Relatives and family friends often pinched my rounded cheeks with the same little jibe every chubby kid hears. "Oh, but she has such a pretty face." If only was left unsaid.

Many times I'd come home to my safe harbor and release my pent up sobs. I soon learned to turn the other cheek to the slurs, name-calling and the usual cruelty saved for those not fitting the accepted mold. The playful little sprites that skipped across the playground, popular with everyone, clearly marked me a pariah. The last to be picked for dodge ball but most commonly the first pelted painfully with the hard rubber ball. I would sit on the sidelines with tears leaving muddy trails on my dirt-smudged face, desperately trying to hide my humiliation.

The middle school years loomed heavily on the horizon. I continually looked forward to the three months of summer vacation and freedom from school. However, this particular summer was the season of change—at least for me. Just before my eleventh birthday in June, the inevitable metamorphosis that changes a girl into a woman suddenly happened. Ah, the mysteries of life.

I had been sent to stay with my grandparents for a week during the summer while my parents enjoyed some rare "alone time." Although my grandparents had raised four girls of their own, I was the oldest granddaughter and it was during this visit my period started for the very first time. The entire household erupted into sudden turmoil. My grandfather was dispatched immediately to the local drugstore. He returned with three grocery bags filled with feminine hygiene products. Mother and I had had the talk and she'd given me a booklet explaining the details of this unsavory rite of passage. I knew what to expect but now faced with three grocery bags, I was scared beyond reason. I wanted to cry. I wanted my mama.

The bags contained: a sanitary belt (ask any woman forty or older, they'll know about these contraptions), maxi pads, medium pads, mini-pads, tampons, douche, a hot water bottle (talk to the same forty-year-old), aspirin, tea bags, granny panties with little hooks to attach the pads, and a bottle of wine. I was slightly confused to say the least. Grandmother put me in a soothing warm bath, handed me a cup of hot tea and aspirin for the cramping, which I really was not experiencing. I wondered if somehow my body wasn't functioning quite right. After my soaking, I was swaddled into a warm terry cloth robe and introduced to the other products.

The tampons were out of question, shame on Granddaddy, those things were only for married women, according to my grandmother! I was snuggly tucked into bed with the hot water bottle and a little taste of the wine (also for the cramping)—one happy girl. Of course, later I was to find out why all the other girls called the dreaded monthly visitor, "the curse". Perhaps that's another story for another time.

Several mysterious things began to happen to my body that summer as well. I developed boobs and grew taller! I had come to the threshold of puberty and crossed to the other side. Except for the obvious changes, I was totally oblivious to the apparent transformation. School began again in September and suddenly I realized life as I knew it had changed.

I took the road of least resistance by joining the band for no other reason than to avoid P.E. class. I really had very little in the way of talent for any instrument, although I tried the entire woodwind section over the coming years. I learned that menstruation could get you out of all sorts of things you didn't want to do, especially if you had a male teacher. Gradually, over the next year, armed with my newly developed body, I began to notice boys from a new perspective and they began to notice me.

Mother took me to a local doctor who had no problem dispensing "diet pills" to anyone who asked for them, thus my first experience with chemical dieting began. The little yellow capsules were guaranteed to rid me of the clinging "baby fat." It was then I began believing in miracle diets which were guaranteed to solve all of life's problems.

I lost weight and for one glorious year, I was well-proportioned. I developed a few friendships and started "going with" a boy in my class. Mother always laughed at that phrase, "just where were we going?" We met at the movies on Friday nights and held hands through the feature, went to school events together, and passed notes in class. That was the extent of it. I do remember one lightning quick peck on the lips we shared in the class supply closet in the fifth grade. We were really embarrassed by the flash of puppy love passion. I felt like I had done something very wrong but on the other hand, it was exciting and made me feel kinda grown-up. I was delighted with the newly gained popularity in school. However, as I continued to watch the bathroom scale, in my heart I felt my new found fame would never last. I loved the attention but my fat alter ego was simply dormant, waiting to emerge once again.

Everyone with a weight problem has tried diet pills in one form or another. Over the counter diet pills—there are hundreds of them, all promising to work magic on your body. Eat anything and still lose weight. Yeah right, sell me some beach-front property in the Sahara. Mother continued to stay on my butt, more aggressively with every pound that padded my frame. My lifelong battle of the bulge was a constant every day happening.

The pills made me feel nervous, jittery, but I did have more energy. Nausea was a tolerated side affect. When I didn't see results immediately, I decided to add laxatives to my daily routine. The idea was at the advice of my best friend who was older than me by five months. She was advised by older sisters, who had "been there, done that." My best buddy and I were in on this diet pill thing together. I think that was the bond that held us together. We were two pre-teen girls who wanted more than anything to be popular.

This was at a time, the late sixties, when doctors freely dispensed pills. No one had ever heard of anorexia or bulimia. I lost weight. What was the damage to my body? I was medicated with massive quantities of caffeine. My heart raced as if the organ was going to spew forth from my newly-gained bosom. I freely admit the morning buzz was a nice high. Soon I was taking two or three pills at a time and staying awake for days on end. The pill habit was not a very healthy life style for a kid who desperately wanted only to fit in with her peers.

When Mother felt I had lost enough weight, she simply took the pills away. I was addicted, of course. I had no idea what was happening to me. I searched the entire house until I found the prescription bottle tucked away in her underwear drawer. When the pill bottle was empty, I panicked. Several days passed before I began to feel better. Going through withdrawal symptoms made me feel deathly ill. Thoughts of suicide flashed through my mind. Luckily, I didn't have the means or the opportunity to make ending my life an option. My story could have ended very abruptly.

My parents had no idea what I was going through. We were a normal every day family. Daddy worked full time at a box factory and when he wasn't at work, he worked our farm with livestock and crops. He had no clue, no time for the everyday workings of our home, which was traditionally mother's domain. She ran the house with an iron hand and a soft shoulder to cry on. Mother was very involved in her children's lives (my sister was born in 1970) as well as those of her parents, sisters, nephews and nieces. We have a huge extended family and never knew who would be living with us next. At

Mother's side, I learned to cook, entertain, and feed the masses.

My struggle to maintain the weight-loss was a losing battle. The pounds piled on and again my mother pointed out each added ounce. The fact she was the best southern cook on the planet didn't help me combat the rising numbers on the scale.

From an early age I was taught most of life's problems can be therapeutically treated with food. Our clan loves to eat. Everything we do revolves around food. We celebrate with vast buffets, we mourn with massive quantities of food; we eat when we're happy and to fill the void when we're sad. The first question when guests arrive is "what do we serve?" When we travel, "where will we eat?" All holidays surround the extended array of covered dishes. We swear each year to cut back on the food but that never happens. Each family member has a favorite dish and we cook them all. From the day we enter this world, our lives revolve around food.

Daddy began struggling with high blood pressure during my adolescent years. Under the strain of two full time jobs, his doctor gave him a grim prognosis … lose weight or die. He never, to this day, ceases to amaze me. Daddy followed a thousand-calorie a day diet and lost the weight, no problem. He carried a small notebook and stubby pencil in his shirt pocket; the pages smeared with dust from the fields, damp from hours of perspiration on the tractor and carried the odorous scent of diesel fuel. He wrote down every morsel he put in his mouth including his bourbon, which he began mixing with Tab (the only low calorie soda available at that time), the combination had to be disgusting.

I tried the diet too. I managed to maintain my weight somewhat through the next few years. I was not thin by any means. My weight hovered around a hundred seventy pounds. For me, at a grand stature of five foot three, I remained thirty pounds or so overweight during my early teens. I continued to struggle, closely watching every bite with my mother criticizing me terribly when I gained a few pounds.

I don't want to give anyone a bad impression of my mother. I stress the point she loved me dearly. Her greatest fear was that I would go through life unhappy or a social outcast. I had already blazed that trail. Heavier kids become either the class clown or simply a misfit no one would dare befriend. I have never been funny. I never did find a much sought after place with the "in" crowd but eventually discovered a niche for myself. Very few of my friendships lasted beyond high school and I seldom spoke with anyone from my classes after graduation.

By my sixteenth birthday, I had met the man who was to become my husband and became sexually active. I don't condone or advocate this behavior. I was terribly young but I'm being brutally honest here. I certainly do not recommend growing up that fast but, as the saying goes, facts are facts. I still constantly dieted; I tried every fad diet that emerged on the scene. Cabbage soup, all fruit, low calorie, low fat, starvation, excessive exercise, the grapefruit diet, over the counter diet pills, anything that might help me lose weight, I'd try. There were many, many more diets but you get the picture.

I felt that to keep a boyfriend, you had to look a certain way. In fact, my boyfriend, later my husband, had weight issues of his own. He managed to work off his excess weight in less than six months by shear physical labor. He has kept the weight off for over thirty years now. Even today if his weight creeps up a bit he simply cuts back on eating without ever saying a word. Still he has that negative self-image that obesity fosters. I think his body is fantastic. Strangely, he has never thought of me (not even at nearly three hundred pounds) as the obese slob I saw looking back at me from the mirror. Ah, true love is blind, thank God!

I wasn't terribly overweight during my late teen years but certainly not the petite girl I wanted so much to be. I've never felt comfortable in my own skin. I continued to diet in stages, suffered with weak kidneys but otherwise the early teen years were quite ordinary. Well they were until…

Chapter Two

~ *THE ROAD TO MORBID OBESITY* ~

I plunged into a new phase of my life at the tender age of seventeen. The inevitable happened and baby makes three. That sounds like pregnancy just happened upon me, but of course, it was not that simple. It was a teenage goof resulting from haphazard birth control and playing reproductive Russian roulette. Hormones run amuck, teens caught up in the moment.

Life, as I knew it, would never be the same again. I was terribly upset over the whole situation and my parents were distraught, to put it mildly. As far as we were concerned there was only one thing to do: we would get married and have our baby. In our young and naive minds, the situation was far less tragic than my parents seemed to think; in fact, we were rather excited about our new "family." His parents had trod this path before with one of his siblings so even though they were less than pleased, they handled everything very calmly.

My world seemed to change overnight. The situation was stressful at home with my parents. After we married, relations with my family remained strained for a while. As a parent now, I know the pain I must have caused them and I deeply regret hurting them. Yet my story is all too common. I married my high school flame and prepared for an instant family. I was blissfully happy.

I took the swelling belly of pregnancy to mean that I could eat anything and everything I wanted. I simply gorged myself. I packed on eighty pounds because, of course, I was eating for two. I was eating in proportions for two grown overweight people. My pregnancy was completely normal. Typically, for gestation, I had a little morning sickness, a little swelling, and many cravings. I ate an abundance of grape lollipops, large red apples, and pizza; hardly a well-rounded diet. I continued to pack on the weight with foods I had previously denied myself.

During my entire pregnancy, I endured my senior year of high school. I worked part-time and tried to adapt to my new station in life as a wife and mother-to-be. We had no money but we were happy. My school friends, with only two very dear exceptions (you know who you are and I thank you), treated me as though I had committed the most mortal sin. The majority of my so-called "friends", as well as the school faculty, felt that my pregnancy would ruin our graduation ceremony; according to them I did not deserve to walk on stage and receive my diploma. I was irreparably hurt. I felt as though I had earned my place in the ceremony. The struggle to meet this milestone was much harder for me than most of the other carefree students who had no grown-up responsibilities. Those fair weather friends were terribly hypocritical, my situation could have happened to anyone of them.

For once in my life, I stood firm against my fellow students and the school faculty. I was now a complete social outcast. I stood virtually alone to face the cold shoulder. Subjected to constant gossip, loud whispers echoed around me intent on keeping me away from graduation. I was deeply hurt. Nearly thirty years later the memory still haunts me. Of course, that was a lifetime ago. Many bridges have been crossed and burned since then. Let bygones be bygones, right. Forgive, sure; forget, yeah, right.

I didn't realize by feeding this baby so well invitro that I would be giving birth to a toddler. I had fed him very well and he grew in proportion. He was a very large, very healthy baby boy who had to be guided out of my young, tender womb with forceps. His shoulders were dislocated in order to deliver him. I had stitches from stem to stern to make way for our new bundle of joy. He was truly the most beautiful baby I had ever seen, named for both of his grandfather's, he was—and is—the light of my life. He was worth every slur, every hard-ship, and any problems we encountered along the way.

He came bounding into our lives on the day I reached my eighteenth birthday. Happy Birthday to me! Happy Birthday to me! From that day forward, the day belonged to the baby. Even to my parents, it was his day. As much as they had stressed over my youthful pregnancy, my parent's love for their first grandson was unconditional and overabundant. They were crazy for that kid. The only person less than pleased was my sister who had been the baby of our family and the apple of my parent's eye. She now had to share the spotlight and was not happy about it at all. Who could blame her, she was only ten? Our family dynamic had experienced a drastic up-heaval because of our new baby and my sister was in the crossfire. I'm so sorry for that pain in her life. Unfortunately, I didn't see it then.

Sadly, I retained most of the "baby" weight. For the first time in my life, I weighed over two hundred pounds. I was so thrilled with our beautiful baby boy the weight went com-pletely unnoticed. I justified the weight, in my mind, as simply baby fat. Surely, the post pregnancy bulk would go away like magic. I was trying to be the best mommy in the world, de-termined to do everything right for my baby boy. I didn't have the time, nor did I really care about the weight. I had many other more important things to occupy my mind.

By the time I did take notice, I had loaded on additional poundage. The up and down of the fluctuating scale would make you dizzy. I embarked on various diets as I gained, lost, and regained literally hundreds of pounds in the next few years. I eventually fell into a dark depression and continued down the destructive path of overindulgence to fill the void. Nothing seemed to work.

I was ashamed of how I looked. I hated the ever-growing fat. I felt unattractive and bloated but my husband seemed to love me no matter what. Strangely, he never saw the weight, only the woman I am at heart. I could not accept myself. I eventually found another pill doctor and used over the counter diet pills, water pills, and laxatives. Nothing ever worked. In-tellectually, I knew the key was to eat less, exercise more, drink water, and do not cheat. Moderation is the most difficult diet of them all. We all long for that instant "melt the fat away" miracle that will never come.

In 1985, I had to have emergency kidney surgery to remove a lodged kidney stone and repair the internal bleeding that followed. The antibiotics given after surgery rendered my birth control pills useless. I'm sure somewhere in the fine print that came in the packet of pills it explains that antibiotics nullify the pills, but who reads those little inserts? Obviously, I didn't. Thus, our youngest son was conceived. It was a shocking surprise but after five years it was time for a new baby and God had brought him to us.

I was extremely active during the pregnancy. This time I gained very little weight and all of it seemed to be baby. Another toddler-sized baby boy was born to us without much difficulty. Unfortunately, this baby boy came with a few problems. He was born with a birth defect it would take the next two years of our lives to get a doctor to recognize that he had a problem.

Worry for our newly born bundle of joy, and the rigors of motherhood, took their toll on my body once more. I packed on still more weight and it just kept piling up. I am and will always be an emotional eater. Name an emotion and I will put together a great menu. I sat home, raising my children and eating. I took odd jobs now and then, most of them involving food somehow. I worked in a grocery store bakery, catered weddings, decorated specialty cakes, and baked pastry as well as inspecting peanuts. I was a closet eater, hiding away and stuffing myself, no one but me and my wardrobe knew how much I actually ate. I would gorge myself on food and then eat entire meals. I had inherited some of my mother's talents in the kitchen. Believe me, I can put together a meal!

We struggled the next few years to find a doctor to tell us just what was wrong with our baby. Finally, when he was two-years-old his problems were finally diagnosed. He was "legally blind." Our baby could distinguish shapes but little else. We worked with him continually, determined not to handicap him further by over protection. Now that he is in his twenties, I'm happy to say he's a well-adjusted, great kid. I couldn't love my beautiful baby more; he was—and continues to be—truly a precious gift.

With my husband's encouragement (well, it was more like shove), I managed to land a good civil service job. I was at my all time highest weight to date of around two hundred thirty pounds. I jumped into the new job with gusto. I felt good about my station in life for the first time in a very long time. I tried to accept myself for the person I was inside and for a while, I did. The job was great and I dearly loved it. I made half attempts to control my weight but for the most part ignored it for a time.

About six months after landing the job, my gall bladder went bad. The offending organ was out of there. It was awful. From that time forward, I suffered from acid reflux but responded well to medication. I had to relearn how to eat because my body reacted adversely to certain foods. I managed my diet pretty well but the change didn't last. Soon I began to eat compulsively once again.

It was in this "real" job with civil service that I heard the words gastric by-pass for the first time. A woman in my office had undergone the surgery years before and although she still appeared to be somewhat overweight, when she finally showed me her "before" pictures I was flabbergasted. She had lost over one hundred pounds and compared to her pre-surgery body she looked fantastic. Her surgery had come with a price. She was unable to eat certain foods, especially lettuce and roughage which caused instant reactions including vomiting and sudden onset diarrhea. I watched her go through times of agony when she cheated. I still couldn't see beyond the one hundred pounds lost. The price seemed to be minimal compared to the weight-loss. I eventually learned how wrong that thinking truly was. When I finally discovered the truth, it was ironic this early warning signal had gone unheeded. The revelation was still years away for me.

Two years later, my world fell apart when my husband and I separated. This was by far the most tragic thing to happen in my life up to that point. Nothing could compare with the pain I felt. We simply were so involved with separate lives that we neglected our relationship. Neither one of us was totally at fault; there was tremendous hurt inflicted on both sides. The most pronounced lesson I learned was that no one knows how he/she will react to any given situation until faced with the circumstance; and no matter how bad things seem there is always something worse. Always. Count your blessings every day.

Strangely enough during our separation, I didn't resort to food to soothe my broken heart. Instead, I leaned on something much more toxic. My diet soon consisted of alcohol, coffee, and cigarettes. It was a hell of a diet and therapy program. I lost weight and looked darn good. The alcohol numbed my emotions, cigarettes helped to calm my nerves but obviously I gave up one compulsive behavior for another. This way of life lasted for two very long years.

I would be lying if I said this was all bad. I had never experienced "single" life as an adult. I sowed some wild oats, nothing too wild, that's just not my style. Ultimately, I still dearly loved my husband and missed him terribly. He was and still is the half that makes me whole. There was no easy answer here and it was an extremely hard road to find our way back to each other again. Eventually we worked out some of the most pressing problems and finally reunited. I set out to become the happy homemaker again. I cooked, baked, fed my family very well, and my weight ballooned once again.

For several years, marriage was a difficult process. Trust was a major factor; however, we managed to reestablish that faith in each other and to move forward. We were both willing to do the work, emerging with a bond to each other stronger than it had ever been. This paragraph is so simplistic compared to how hard this period was to endure. The key to this dilemma was that both he and I wanted our marriage to work.

During the separation, I moved with our kids to the Georgia coast. I had always dreamed of being near the ocean. The community is small but I love it. Once we were reunited, my husband quit his job and joined us on the coast. His former job had nearly cost us our marriage. It had required extensive hours, most of them on the road and away from home. There were times when the only way I knew he'd been home were his dirty socks on the living room floor. He'd be gone by the time I woke up in the mornings and not return home until after I was asleep at night. We were leading separate lives. To survive, we started all over again. We vowed never to let outside pressures come before our relationship and to spend a portion of everyday simply sharing our lives. He started his own business. It was difficult but we have made it a success. I still worked civil service, which provided a steady paycheck and benefits.

It was here in our new found hometown that we began to entertain. Frequently our house was the home base for parties. I cooked enormous buffets. Sunday football parties were a common occasion at our home. I would feed twenty to thirty people on any given weekend during the summer and fall months. I became the hostess of our group and put together some great gala events.

We scrimped and saved to purchase our first "real" home. I have never felt so fulfilled. We were now homeowners, had a relatively happy marriage, the kids were being kids, and we were developing a new social life. We expanded our social circle and it was at this point that a dear friend first came into my life. She has been by my side through thick and thin. It is hard to imagine how I could have gotten through the most difficult times of my life without her.

We entertained in our new home and as consistent with my life, I cooked a lot. I should have been happy, after all I had everything I'd ever wanted, and still I could not accept the fat girl persona. I was uncomfortable with my looks and myself. I weighed an all time high of two hundred forty pounds. I have always tried to dress nicely, however it was difficult to look nice in "woman size" clothes, nothing was ever stylish or sheik. My self-loathing can only be understood by those who have walked the path of obesity. I feel guilty making these admissions because I know so many who have dealt with the same issues. I'm aware that many have dealt with much greater weight problems than I have, their sorrow and heart-wrenching stories are surely more intense than mine. None-the-less I knew the pain of obesity. The weight masked the person I wanted to be and trapped me inside a body from which I could find no escape. I put on a good act. My self-esteem was at an all time low at this point in my life and I felt as if I were sinking steadily into deeper, darker depression day by day.

My sister is one of those women who have struggled with much more weight than I've ever dealt with. I never could understand how she always looked so beautifully put together. She is truly a beautiful person, both her inner and outward appearance. Her story is much the same as mine with some variations. I could always sympathize with her but never can claim to know the depth of her despair. In fact, it was her mention of gastric by-pass surgery that really put the idea in my mind, though I have never admitted that to anyone. She had a much different experience with this surgery. Between the two of us, I think we have nearly covered the entire spectrum of possibilities concerning gastric by-pass surgery. I pull from her situation as well as my own as my story unfolds in later chapters, ultimately to view another perspective. As sisters, we're intimately connected, but further, the two of us are great friends. In many ways she inspires me. It is because of this that I have dedicated this book to her.

The most traumatic, devastating event of my life occurred in 1999. Suddenly, with very little warning, our family had to face the serious illness of our beloved mother and her eventual death after more than two agonizing months. This woman was the center of our lives and that of our extended family. Mother's loss changed the entire dynamic of our family. We were plunged into despair that none of us was prepared to experience. The loss of our mother brought my sister and me together, cementing a bond between us that we'd never had before. Even though we were always sisters in the traditional sense of the word, we now developed a wonderful close friendship bringing us to an elevated plane in our relationship. The intense mourning for Mother was a pain common to both of us, even though our own personal connections to her were very different.

I spent the nine weeks of mother's illness, virtually seven days a week, twenty-four hours a day, living in the waiting room of the Cardiac Intensive Care Unit on constant vigil. Other than the hospital cafeteria, which provided balanced meals, though less than appetizing, the only other option was fast food. Unfortunately, the hours the cafeteria served meals coincided with the times that doctors made their rounds. So in order to see the doctors when they examined Mother, eating at the cafeteria was nearly impossible. We had only one option … that of fast food, three-four meals a day. My mind was occupied with Mother's declining health. Diet was the very last thing on my mind.

It was during this time I began to write. There were countless hours we sat in the waiting room with nothing to occupy the time. I have always written, but my parents never encouraged me to take this "hobby" any further and I never really thought I had any talent to pursue it. But I've always found comfort in putting thoughts on paper. I began a historical fiction novel, a genre that I truly love, and it was this project I used to fill the endless hours spent by my mother's side during her last days.

Not that you can measure these things, however, I felt my sister was under more personal stress than I was as we tended our mother. She had a beautiful baby boy who had only recently observed his first birthday. Her life involved caring for the baby, working full-time, and being at the hospital every possible moment. Running back and forth between these demanding responsibilities was tiring and stressful, regular meals were not in the cards for her either. We never discussed it but she probably put on weight during this time as I did, it just wasn't important to either of us then.

We lost mother in May 1999. We mourned in typical fashion. Everyone we knew brought food, tons of food. Our family bore the intense grief gorging on hundreds of dishes, acting almost on remote control. We felt blessed with an abundance of beloved family and friends. The amount of food was enough to feed a small third world country. We managed to get through the worst of times and go on with our lives, though life would never be the same for any of us.

Chapter Three

~ GASTRIC BY-PASS SURGERY RESEARCH ~

I had thought about the gastric by-pass surgery for a long time before I ever began researching the possibility. I mentioned this thought process to no one. I knew very little about what the surgery entailed. I've had quite a number of surgical procedures throughout my life so the prospect of going under the knife was not frightening to me—well maybe a little. However, the thought of a surgery that could resolve my weight problems sounded miraculous, a dream come true. For over a year thoughts of something called a roux en-y gastric by-pass surgery rolled around in my head, though I did nothing to pursue the idea. As always, life happened, the surgery was a looming distant thought, always occupying space in the back of my mind.

I began writing my first book in 1999; it was a work of historical fiction that I had done an enormous amount of research on and in fact finished writing. An editor read the work (yet untitled) and did not give the "book" an encouraging review. I put the work aside and having no self-confidence deemed my writing endeavor an utter failure. Just another project I'd failed in, not really a new concept for me.

As with most worthy things, the idea for my first real book happened upon us when we least expected it. Memorial Day weekend of 2000, my husband and I were camping with friends when he, in fact, proposed a wonderful project that would become my book series called "Get Off The Interstate."

Strangely enough, it was this first book in the series that would spur me into beginning the aggressive research into weight-loss surgery.

"Get Off The Interstate" involves the stories behind state historical markers situated along the Atlantic coastline. I began the series in Georgia, because, of course, that is where we live. Research and writing the first book took a little more than two years. As the actual prospect of the book became a reality, I realized that publicizing a book meant I would have to put myself in the public eye. Because I was so very uncomfortable with my appearance, I soon concluded that weight-loss surgery might be the answer to my prayers. Quietly, I began to look into the surgery, still confiding in no one.

As a writer, research is something I excel at and I began my research with the Internet. Initially I gathered tons of information about the different types of weight-loss surgeries performed at that time. The list of options was brief. The most obvious choice was the *roux-en-y* gastric by-pass. I focused on it. Then getting deep into research, I discovered the latest development with the *roux-en-y* surgery was a minimally evasive technique through the laparoscope. This procedure meant recovery time could be very quick, theoretically, with only three or four very small incisions. I compiled enormous amounts of materials giving the pros and cons of surgery with contrasting points of view.

After gathering a great deal of information, I decided that the laparoscopic *roux-en-y* was the surgery for me. I learned the basic anatomy of the surgery. Simply put, a large portion of the stomach is sectioned off and stapled leaving a small pouch, usually only one to two ounces in size, then additionally approximately two feet of the small intestine is removed, the remainder of the intestine is reconnected to the "new" stomach pouch creating the "y."

Most sources recorded a ten to fifteen percent complication rate, which seemed reasonable to me. Complications usually involved bowel obstructions, leaks in the staple line, risk of hernia, excessive scar tissue and a lowered immune system. The small stomach pouch only allows the patient to consume small quantities of food thus forcing the weight loss. A portion of the intestine is cut away because it is here where the majority of a person's calories are absorbed into the system. However, this is also where vitamins and nutrients are absorbed from the foods we eat; therefore, malabsorption could be a very serious issue as well. Remember the saying, "If I knew then, what I know now?"

Patients receive counseling, in most cases, that in order to avoid the risk of malabsorption, vitamins and nutritional supplements would become necessary for the rest of your life. Everything I had learned seemed acceptable. Of course, there were the usual risks involving any surgery, the chance of infection and complications from anesthesia. I had faced these possibilities many times before and knew them well.

I discovered that for *roux-en-y* gastric by-pass insurance approval, the patient must be at least one hundred pounds overweight. I would be cutting that restriction close. In addition, my insurance required that a candidate for surgery must have at least two co-morbidities. Okay, so what was that? I found that these were health problems resulting directly from obesity. The illnesses were frequently diabetes, high blood pressure, thyroid problems, acid reflux, joint stress, and a host of others. I had severe gastric reflux, joint stress on my knees and ankles, and thyroid problems so this first hurdle was easy. Still, I was just under the one hundred-pound weight requirement. That fact did not deter me. Like Scarlett in "Gone with the Wind," I would think about that tomorrow.

Through a great website, I found quite a few people living within fifty miles of us who had elected to have the surgery. I emailed each one, all of whom were women. I had so many questions and anxiously awaited responses. Of twenty-eight emails I sent, I received sixteen replies. Almost everyone was very forthcoming with advice, having distinct answers to my probing questions. How much weight had they lost, did they have complications, what doctor did they use, what could they eat now and how much, how was their health, how painful was the surgery, how long did it take to recover, how do they feel now? Only someone who had experienced the surgery could address my concerns. Everyone I spoke with was more than willing to offer advice based on their own personal experiences.

The major hurdle seemed to be relearning how to eat. Dumping, that's gastric by-pass speak for vomiting or diarrhea, was common to every patient and quite frequent. The patients I consulted presented an all around rosy picture, though I realize now I was only listening to the good parts and discounted anything negative, I just didn't want to hear it. All of the individuals would have the surgery over again if given the option. Everyone had experienced some sort of complication, although most problems seemed minor.

Several of the women had used a doctor about forty miles to the south of my home. From all reports, he was a good doctor but very strict. He required all of his patients to lose twenty percent of their excess weight before he'd agree to perform the surgery. In addition, patients were to complete an intensive pre-surgery (and very expensive) lecture series preparing them for the change that weight-loss surgery would bring to their lives. I will freely admit this doctor intimidated me. He seemed to be terribly demanding. As far as his insistence that all patients lose twenty percent of their weight in advance, I thought this was ludicrous. If I could lose the weight on my own then why would I consider the surgery?

My sister had chosen to have the surgery using a doctor who did nothing but gastric by-pass. The fact that he was located in north Georgia was good for her. I was very impressed with the program this doctor offered, according to what I'd read on his extensive website. My major objection was the fact he was more than seven hours from my home and I just didn't want to have surgery that far away. I had read of people traveling to different states by airplane to use a certain doctor, this option was not for me. However, I was very pleased my sister would be in the hands of this seemingly very capable doctor. I even went with her for a consultation, to continue my research.

By this time I had confided in my sister and a friend. Still, I was hesitant about talking to my husband. I knew in my heart he'd disapprove. I realized I couldn't continue this process without discussing my intent with the most important person in my life. I was right about his reaction but luckily, he didn't immediately dismiss the idea and kept an open mind. I was relieved the idea of surgery didn't result in the disagreement between us. As always, he only wanted me healthy and happy. Relieved, I now felt I could move forward.

The next step began with my health insurance company. I was elated to discover that given the standard qualifications, they would approve the surgery. The company provided a list of preferred providers or doctors, who participated in my insurance plan. I began collecting data on each of the doctors on the list who were within fifty miles of our home, roughly an hour's drive. Of course, I'd already eliminated the one doctor, leaving only three others. I began by questioning patients who had used these surgeons.

I invited the women who had undergone the surgery to lunch, one by one. Not only could I meet them face to face to see their weight-loss first hand, discuss their experiences, I could also watch them eat. I realize this might sound somewhat strange but I wanted to know exactly how my meals and eating habits would have to change. I was amazed at how forth coming everyone seemed to be. It was as if I were joining a very different kind of sorority. The members were anxious to encourage others to join. Later, I was to learn just how high the dues to join this group could be.

I was determined to get as much detail as possible concerning what was in store for me should I decide to have the surgery. Really, it was a forgone conclusion, I'd already made up my mind but felt in order to sell the idea to those who love me, I'd have to gather some very convincing evidence.

The most common complaint seemed to be throwing up or dumping after eating sweets, overeating, eating too fast or just consuming something which didn't agree with their newly-constructed pouch. Bouts of diarrhea, painful gas and losing hair from protein deficiency came up in conversation frequently. Everyone had a little different perspective and variation of what they could eat and how much. Unanimously, all agreed the surgery was well worth any of the bad experiences.

Each person had lost more than one hundred pounds; one woman had initially weighed over four hundred pounds and had now shrunk to an amazing one hundred sixty pounds.

Several of the women were considering plastic surgery to remove excess skin and tighten up their now svelte bodies. I disregarded that information completely; I'm not sure exactly why but it didn't seem to be an issue for me.

Determined to leave no questions in my mind, I forced myself to read the accounts of patients who had passed away after having weight-loss surgery. I read with tears in my eyes of patients who never realized their dream. The majority of these were severely obese, over five hundred pounds, with life threatening health concerns in addition to the weight. Knowing this, I put the fear of death completely out of my mind. Only a very small number of patients reportedly died due to direct complications of the surgery itself. My mind was relieved, yet little did I know the wide range of complications that were totally discounted as having nothing to do with gastric by-pass surgery. Many of the complications had resulted in death and oddly enough suicides.

My husband was well aware of my long fought battle with weight, yet still he felt this solution was too extreme. He was much more concerned with my well being than with the way I looked, weight was never an issue for him as far as I was concerned. I know his eyes remained clouded by love, yet I could only see a fat face looking back at me from the mirror. Regardless of his apprehension, my husband extended his full support, but just short of encouragement. He had questions that only a surgeon could answer, although I felt that after all my research I knew all I needed to know. My husband held his opinions in reserve until I took this a step further and made an appointment to meet with a surgeon who actually performed the *roux-en-y* gastric by-pass.

It was frustrating for me. Why didn't he just believe what I was telling him? My husband wasn't that easily convinced. My best friend didn't really understand. All she could see was the pain in store for me; she too, only looked toward my well being. My sister, on the other hand, completely got it. She was thrilled for me as well as the fact we would be going through this process together. We had yet to know how different our experiences would be. I was on the verge of stepping off a cliff and didn't even know it.

Chapter Four

~ THE NEXT STEP ~

The next step involved getting my ducks in a row. I had amassed reams of paper extolling the virtues of gastric by-pass surgery. I now had a circle of friends who were in various stages of the gastric by-pass process. We tried to form a local support group for those in our area that belonged to this specific clique. I had yet to have surgery or even speak to a physician about the possibility of surgery. Here I was jumping into this plan with both feet. The support group never did get off the ground.

In order to cover all my bases, I made an appointment with our family doctor to discuss the idea of weight-loss surgery. I was shocked at her response. She was well aware of the constant war I had waged with the battle of the bulge and over the years had prescribed various medications, given me various diets to follow and warned me repeatedly about the rising numbers on the scale. No diet had worked for more than a brief period then I would regain the weight plus a few more pounds. She was adamant; gastric by-pass surgery was a bad idea. I left her office feeling totally depressed.

Yet, I still refused to allow any negativity toward the surgery deter me. I justified obstacles intellectually as unfair bias against the procedure. I felt disappointed by our family doctor's reaction to my plans. I longed for unanimous approval. I realize now that my doctor, who knew me so well, only had my best interest at heart. Hindsight is indeed twenty-twenty.

Her reason against the surgery concerned the risk factor

and more often than not, an excessive rate of moderate to serious complications. She reasoned that the surgery did nothing to modify the behavior that resulted in the obesity to begin with. Further, I was not a candidate for surgery based on the insurance stipulation that I be one hundred pounds above my "ideal" weight. The doctor's reasoning went on and on as she fervently impressed upon me that gastric by-pass surgery was simply too dangerous. Stubbornly, I refused to heed her warnings. I had made up my mind. I would not allow anything or anyone to stand in my way at this point.

Some small portion of my psyche continued to nag me with doubt. I forced myself to examine all aspects of the surgery once again to ensure that I was fully informed. I closely scrutinized a very popular website covering every aspect of this process. I again read the obituaries of those who had, for various reasons, not survived. The experience was sobering, leaving me with depressingly morbid thoughts. Still I held firm to the attitude that these results "will never happen to me." In an attempt to "talk" myself out of having the surgery, I immersed myself in the dreadful possibilities of complications and death. The diversion was only temporary.

I remained close to my surgery sorority sisters, basking in their encouragement. Ultimately, my desire to be a "normal" size far outweighed any negativity. I didn't dare hope for an attractive figure. I didn't consider what effect this would have on my family and friends or even my health. Of course, the majority of individuals who consider weight-loss surgery spout the same "politically correct" verbiage; their health is the primary concern.

On the top ten lists of reasons in favor of surgery, "health" is probably number four behind being attractive, socially acceptable, and a boost in self-esteem. Personally, I wanted self-confidence. I wanted to be attractive. I wanted to tie my shoes and wipe my own backside without straining. You might find that statement to be quite vulgar; however, that is the reality of obesity. I hated being the largest person in the room and the entire stigma that followed.

I have never felt good about my body. I am unable to see beyond the mirror's image, therefore I find myself lacking at every turn. Erroneously, I believed being thin would solve all of life's problems. I have always found it strange that my best friend, who is one hundred ten pounds or so, has issues with her body. She exercises like a fiend and is always in constant motion in order to maintain her weight. She was terribly upset that I was resorting to surgery to lose weight because she'd always seen me through loving eyes and was only concerned for my well-being. In fact, I believe, my best friend was probably the most upset with my decision to have gastric bypass surgery.

Weighing all of the aspects (no pun intended), I made the final decision to go ahead with my plans and finally took the long awaited first step in my journey. Armed with my meticulously gathered data I chose a surgeon located approximately forty miles north of our home and called for an appointment. The date was set for the next month and the suspense was killing me. I could hardly contain my excitement. The first official step toward surgery was completed. I knew my life was going to be forever changed but I had no idea to what extent.

I was, of course, first exposed to the doctor's staff and as with most impressions, this one was very important. I was impressed; they answered every preliminary question I had over the phone. Several days later, I received an extensive packet of paperwork. The thick packet was to be read then completed prior to my appointment. Opening the envelope was like ripping off gift-wrapping on Christmas morning. I could hardly contain my excitement.

The paperwork would lay bare my entire life history with answering this battery of questions. The paperwork included complete medical history forms, a record of various attempts to lose weight, the standard personal information as well as insurance coverage. I compiled a list of questions as I read through the packet concerning items I would like the surgeon to clarify. As the date of the appointment grew near, I experienced a myriad of emotions, spanning from nervousness to elation. My husband planned to accompany me to the initial consultation because he also had questions he wanted answered. His questions were by far tougher than mine.

As the cool winter morning of my appointment approached, I began having second thoughts. I'd read a brief article stating that gastric by-pass patients have a shortened life expectancy due to the extensive changes to the body's anatomy and physiology. I didn't read the entire article because that phrase had hit me like a ton of bricks. In fact, that passage still haunts me to this day. I told no one at that time or since.

I carefully dressed for my appointment, changing clothes at least three times. We set out on the early morning trip north, the address was easy to find. We spoke not a word on the forty-five minute drive. As we waited for my name to be called we continued in silence. I glanced around the room, careful not to stare, taking in the patient obviously in various stages of the process. I wanted to ask everyone in the waiting room about his or her experience. But not a sound was uttered in the room and I dare not break the deafening silence.

When the nurse called my name, I was startled; bouncing up like my butt was set on a spring. The first stop was the dreaded scale only this time I was hoping to have gained weight rather than lost so that I would qualify for the surgery. Weighing in, I suddenly realized that in all the years of our marriage, I had never admitted to my actual weight to my husband. He was completely unfazed by the two hundred twenty-seven pounds the evil scale announced. I was embarrassed. I outweighed him by nearly thirty pounds yet I had hoped to put on a little more poundage to ensure I met the insurance weight requirement for the insurance approval.

After the usual procedure temperature, pulse, blood pressure, we sat alone in silence waiting for our turn with the doctor. Maybe it was fear or nervousness, but the room seemed to be closing in around me. As claustrophobia gripped my mind, I found it hard to catch my breath. It dawned on me that I was having an anxiety attack. I mentally tried to calm myself. Concentrate, breathe deeply, calm, calm, calm… bull… I was scared to death.

The doctor came whirling in, as if he had some quota to meet at the end of day. As he introduced himself, I noticed he seemed older than I expected, smaller in stature and wore a slightly unshaven scruff. I felt slightly put off by his appearance and demeanor; I accepted that he was simply not what I had imagined. Without further ado, he plunged into the surgical process of gastric by-pass. He began detailing the roux en-y as if having the surgery was a forgone conclusion. True, I had made up my mind to have the surgery but I didn't expect the doctor to be so abrupt.

I asked the questions I had carefully prepared. Although he addressed some of my concerns, many topics were side-stepped quite gracefully. The one question looming large in my husband's mind was, "if there were complications, could this procedure be reversed?" We were confidently assured that if needed, a reversal surgery, though complicated, was completely possible … no worries there.

The doctor aggressively began to "sell" us the option of laparoscopic surgery rather than the open procedure commonly done. He informed me that although he hadn't performed the laparoscopic surgery as yet that over the course of the next week, he, in fact, was traveling to California to train in the technique. He launched into an enthusiastic high pressure sales pitch. I declined the offer to be his first laparoscopic attempt. The disappointment was unmasked on the doctor's face, almost as if my refusal had insulted him personally. Again, I set those feelings aside.

As our appointment ended, the doctor instructed me to go home and gain at least twenty-five pounds so that I clearly met the weight requirement for insurance coverage. I had documented evidence of co-morbidities including severe gastric reflux, edema (swelling of the hands and feet), thyroid problems, and joint pain so that hurdle was not a problem. The doctor seemed to be going through the motions with no personal interest whatsoever. I was one patient on the assembly line of his practice. The office would file my insurance and once approved we could go forward with the other formalities required for surgery. "Sign the paperwork to obtain pre-approval from the insurance and we will call you when we receive a reply, approval could take anywhere from two to six weeks. Have a good day, good bye." With that, the whirling dervish that was my soon-to-be surgeon left the room. Were it not for the surgeon's kind and caring staff, I would've been very disappointed with my visit.

In hindsight, alarm bells should have gone off in my brain. Human nature allows us to disregard the conversation we do not want to hear. I was in nearly complete denial; I refused to allow common sense overcome determination. The doctor had in fact performed less than fifty surgeries, his practice did not include an aftercare program, and his personality was cold and brusque. Had I been thinking clearly without the veil of desperation to be "normal", I would've walked out of the office that day and never looked back. Instead, I accepted my misgivings, attributing them to nervousness and emotion, and then forged blindly ahead.

We returned home to await the insurance company's decision. I realize now that the doctor, in order to get insurance approval, had to lie about my weight by more than twenty pounds. Still, as instructed, I ate everything in sight to gain weight. A license to pack on the pounds and I took full advantage of it by gorging myself on every favorite food and lots of it. When you want to gain weight, it's not as easy. This process certainly was not natural instinct for me, but I managed to pig-out all the same.

During this time, I was so busy I really didn't have time to dread the wait. I was in the process of completing my first book, working full time, managing a home, and trying to keep up with our two sons. I gave my supervisor notice that, if approved, I planned to have surgery. Because my job was sedentary, I would probably be out of work for a total of four weeks. I had enough vacation time for two weeks paid leave but the remainder of the time would be unpaid. Because my husband was self-employed, his work was often sporadic. We hadn't depended on his income for the past ten years, so now we would rely on his income heavily. I managed to set aside money to tide us over for the short time I'd be on leave without pay. I prepared my official request for the leave of absence then waited for the final word from the insurance company.

I began concentrating every spare moment into the completion of my first book. After all, this book was the catalyst driving me toward the surgery. I was so proud of the book, I wanted to feel confident presenting it to the public. Though appearance didn't seem to matter to anyone but me, this is the way I felt deep in my heart. I knew I'd be down but not out after surgery so the "recovery" time would give me ample opportunity to finish final preparations for print. I was set, ready to move forward. I never realized how long I could actually hold my breath!

I never discussed the prospect of surgery with our children. I suppose I had never considered them the "adult men" they had become. They were still my babies that I would protect with my life. I didn't understand until much later they were so very worried for me. Coupled with the fact they'd lost their dear grandma suddenly in 1999, the boys were terrified that I might leave them as well. Yet, the boys said nothing. I should have spoken with them; both of them were certainly old enough to understand but I never did.

It was a Thursday, February 28, 2002. I had been to lunch with the guys I worked with (thirteen inspectors and engineers, I was their queen and they made me feel like it too!). When I arrived back in my office, there was a message from my husband on my voice mail. Very calmly, he recorded on my office answering machine, that the doctor's office had called and I should call them back this afternoon. I frantically dialed our home number "What exactly did they say? Did they sound negative? Was I approved?" He nonchalantly replied they'd said nothing further, just to return the call. I know he was deeply concerned about the surgery yet he tried to appear very unaffected. This reaction was common for my husband regarding emotions, reveal nothing. I mentally prepared for an expected fight with the insurance company and steeled my self for a negative answer as I dialed the phone.

I dialed the first few numbers then hung up. With my head in my hands, tears rolled down my cheeks. I knew this phone call would likely change my life. Now that the moment was upon me, I was terrified to hear the final verdict. Should approval for the surgery be denied, I would immediately launch into the appeals process. I sat completely still at my desk for more than a half-hour contemplating the entire situation in my mind. I wished my husband was there with me, my sister, my best friend, anyone I loved, to hold my hand through this but I was alone. I walked outside and bummed a cigarette to settle my nerves. This was the first cigarette in more than six months, I had quit in preparation for the surgery. I simply felt I needed something to calm me. I had to sit down when a flush spread through my body as the nicotine coursed to my brain. There are few times in a life where you realize things are about to dramatically change, at this moment I had that sort of epiphany. I was genuinely terrified for the first time in this long awaited process.

Slowly, I walked back to my desk and gripped the card bearing the doctor's office number. Finally taking a deep breath, I dialed the number again. I had to laugh, now that I had finally garnered enough courage to place the call, the line was busy. I hit the redial button. I continued to punch the re-dial button repeatedly for thirty minutes. I almost hung up, when on the sixth attempt, the phone began to ring. At the second ring, the call finally went through. The receptionist had a pleasant voice. Startled, I could hardly speak. Hoarsely, I identified myself and said I was returning their call. She put me on hold for the nurse. I sat for what seemed like forever listening to dead air, trying to take slow deep breaths to calm my racing heart. The nurse came on the line. I didn't dare breathe.

Chapter Five

~ THE DECISION ~

V alerie, how are you?" She spoke with the enthusiastic voice of a friend. I cautiously responded, "I don't know, you tell me." Then she said the words I had been waiting for "you've been approved." I was stunned into silence. I had steeled myself for a negative answer, armored, ready to wage war with the insurance company. Simple as that. Now I was at a loss with all the steam I had mustered for the fight with the insurance company.

Exactly two weeks and two days from the time the paperwork went in for the surgical pre-approval, I had an approval. Of course, there always seems to be a catch. The insurance company wouldn't commit to a final payment until after the surgery was completed. I was assured this small obstacle was very common, no worries there.

A preliminary appointment was scheduled and I spent the following weekend calling everyone I could think of; my family, friends and all of the gastric by-pass patients who had so graciously supported me. My husband seemed ambivalent. He wanted me to be happy yet he was still convinced this surgery was too drastic and silently he prayed I'd reconsider. Far from that, I was excited to embark on this next phase of my life I could hardly contain myself.

My sister, on the other hand, was overjoyed for me. To accommodate her position as a teacher, my sister's surgery would be in July. It was as if we were going through the experience together and I couldn't imagine sharing it with anyone else. We could support each other through this, fully understanding what the other was going through. Though we would have very different outcomes, she has been there for me through this entire process. My best friend was apprehensive, like my husband, she wanted me to be happy and always loved me unconditionally.

The day before my appointment, as I had many times in the past, I had lunch with one of my gastric by-pass friends. She presented me with a folder of information she'd gathered prior to her surgery. The packet contained everything imaginable from how to stock your pantry to what to pack for your hospital stay. This packet became my surgery bible.

As time passed, I began to obsessively study the information in the folder; it proved to be very valuable information. The information included what to expect after surgery at different time increments, also what I should be eating at each stage as well as examples of how my body might physically and mentally react. There were pages anticipating how others including those closest to me could possibly respond to my metamorphosis. Foolishly, I discounted that information. I believed that ultimately no one in my most intimate circle would experience any changes except maybe my husband. It's amazing how wrong that assumption actually was.

Being practical (and a bit morose), I sat at my desk in preparation for the surgery and completed my living will. I filed one at home for my husband, mailed one to my sister and the other to my best friend. Each one had a note attached indicating the envelope was to be opened in the event of my incapacity or death. I felt as if I had left no detail unattended.

The living will was important to me after the turmoil we'd previously experienced as a family when Mother was dying. I wanted to ensure that in the event of this situation, the decisions would be as easy as possible for my family by spelling out exactly what I desired. Then I set aside all negative feelings. I was young and invincible, right?

My follow-up appointment was the next day, this time I would go it alone. My weight had risen a disappointing eleven pounds. I had done my piggish best to gain weight. Maybe gaining weight was as tough as losing weight; I had no experience with that. My vitals were tested and not surprising, my blood pressure somewhat elevated. It was pure anxiety but for the insurance a notation was made in my chart listing me as hypertensive (which was never the case). The nurse went over my entire medical history, noting every ailment and surgery. It was at this point I realized, in fact, every spare body part with the exception of my appendix was already gone. I had chosen to wear black that day because the color makes one appear thinner. I thought about that as a before picture was snapped for my record. I scrawled my signature on what seemed to be reams of paperwork; insurance forms, permission for surgery, and on and on.

The doctor very briefly came to the examining room door to inform me that my insurance required a psychiatric evaluation and a battery of pre-surgical testing. This was common so I was not surprised. Again, the doctor pressed me to allow him to do the surgery laparoscopically but I stood firm in my decision. He wore a look of pure disgust. It was very evident the surgeon was not happy with me. Why did I not just walk away? I have asked myself repeatedly. At the lowest ebb of my self-esteem, I didn't think I deserved better treatment, sad but an all too true fact concerning many obese people.

The first available surgical date was March 13 in order to complete all pre-surgical requirements. I realized this date would become one of the most important in my life. At this point I had no idea just how drastic my world was about to change.

The doctor left the room without another word. He gave me no opportunity to ask him further questions, gave me no words of encouragement, nothing. He left me sitting on the examining table staring at a closed door with a feeling of bewilderment. Alarm bells and bright flashing lights should have appeared before me, instead, I sat there simply feeling grateful to have been approved. I wouldn't allow one moment of doubt to seep into my brain. My subconscious was shouting at this point, but I set all of the apprehension aside. I refused to deal with anything negative; this was simply bad judgment on my part. I was in complete denial.

Low self-esteem left me with the feeling that not only did

I not deserve better treatment from this surgeon, but that I had no right to expect or demand it. I agonize today over how wrong that thinking truly is; everyone has the right and should expect the best from their health care professionals, everyone.

The nurse returned to give me the name and phone number of the psychiatrist I was to call for my psychological evaluation. The office would call with the date and time I should go to the hospital for pre-admission testing. Kindly she asked if I had any further questions and it was at this point I took the opportunity to inquire about seeing a nutritionist as part of my aftercare. The response startled me. The doctor did not have a nutritionist on staff and if I felt the need to consult someone concerning my nutritional needs, it would be on my own and at my own expense. The surgeon's office couldn't even recommend a nutritionist to consult. The only advice the receptionist or nurse had was to inquire at the hospital if I felt a need for further services. I would not see the doctor again until the day following surgery. Although, his staff was very attentive, the doctor was a huge disappointment. Still I mentally blocked all negative thoughts.

Seeing the doctor outside the exam room, I quickly took the opportunity to ask about aftercare. He responded that I was well-informed. Therefore, in his opinion, I required no further assistance from him. He explained to me that as a surgeon, he was not there to be my friend. Where was his bedside manner, common kindness, or even simple patient care? I couldn't allow my mind to go there. Involuntarily, I shuddered. I focused all of my energy on the surgery ahead.

I swallowed my apprehension and forged on. The next step involved getting an appointment for the psychiatric evaluation. I have an inherent distrust for "head" doctors. It seems that without exception when a physician cannot quite identify symptoms, a diagnosis of emotional issues results. All of my life I was intermittently taught to believe emotional problems were a sign of weakness, therefore, I developed a great aversion to anything involving mental health.

I set aside my preconceived notions and called for an appointment with the psychiatrist. Two days later, I found myself sitting in a waiting room surrounded by a herd of unruly children. I wondered if I was in the right place, as I signed in I realized that in fact I was. The wait seemed like hours as these loud, undisciplined kids ran around, jumping off the furniture like little heathens while their mother sat unfazed reading a magazine. I have noticed I am less and less tolerant of screaming children, as I grow older. I finally heard my name called after a tortuous forty-five minute wait. As I walked into the counselor's office, I could feel a stress headache banging away at my temples. I was ushered into a comfortable living-room setting and introduced to the psychiatrist assigned to do my brain probe.

Her questions were personal and thought provoking, delving into all aspects of my life from my childhood through the years of my marriage. As usually is the case, I couldn't stop myself from revealing my entire life's story leaving no stone unturned. I have often felt I expose myself all too freely. I have always been an open book. I don't seem to tolerate secrets very well. By the end of my session, I was totally unburdened and pronounced mentally acute, at least that's what the counselor said. Surprisingly, I was told to return the following day for a five hundred-question written evaluation. I was stunned. I was under the impression that with the one appointment, the psychiatrist would either bind me in a straight jacket or she'd sign off on the paperwork and I would go forward in the pursuit of surgery. Obviously, it wasn't quite that easy.

I did return the following day. The questions ranged from simple reactions to in depth inquiries of morality and values. I felt this evaluation was ridiculous but I sat through it regardless as a means to achieve my primary goal. I don't know if I passed the exam, maybe it wasn't a simple pass/fail type situation or simply a paperwork shuffle, who knows. I assume I passed muster because the schedule for surgery never wavered and I never saw or heard from this psychiatrist again.

The surgeon's receptionist called and told me to report to the hospital on March 11 for pre-surgical testing. Of course, this came with the familiar mantra, nothing to eat or drink after midnight. I'd love to have a dime for every time I've heard that, I'd be rich!

At the hospital I was X-rayed from stem to stern, blood taken (it seemed like nearly all of it) and I spoke to an anesthesiologist. I returned to radiology where I drank a thick white barium milkshake. It was so dry calling the thing a drink was a stretch. The awful concoction tasted like what I imagined a stick of chalk might if anyone was so daft as to eat it. Every bit of moisture in my mouth and throat dried to the point I thought I might spew dust. After another series of X-rays, I was free to go with a warning I should drink as much water as possible to flush the barium from my body. A mental image of bowels filled with concrete flashed through my mind. It was not a pleasing insight.

The day of surgery was looming near on the horizon and I was determined to do everything right. I carefully prepared my bag for the hospital, literally checking off the items on my suggested list. As I am prone to do, I made endless lists making sure no task was undone. I noted what groceries to buy, people my husband should call after the surgery, and so on. I clung to my surgery folder like a lifeline. As I completed each detail, I checked them off my list.

I truly believe had I not done the extensive research on the surgery, I would've entered into the procedure totally lost. I like a certain order to my life and being in control of my fate is very important to me. So much was lacking in my surgeon's care. I was as ready as I could be to undertake the next step in this voyage. It was surgery eve and I enjoyed my "last supper" of steak, baked potato, salad, and cheesecake. Before lying down for a restless night, I prayed for an easy surgery, no complications, and a quick recovery. I was placing my life in the hands of this uncaring surgeon and leaving the rest up to God. God had his job cut out for him, it would be a long hard road, but indeed he had a plan; I just was not privy to it.

Chapter Six

~ SURGERY ~

I spent a sleepless night tossing and turning, knowing my alarm would begin to squawk at six o'clock in the morning. The details of surgery kept cycling through my brain. I prayed everything would go well and asked Mama see me through this (my faith told me God was with me, but I wanted my mama, too.) Every item on my endless lists had been neatly ticked off. My suitcase was packed and by the door. My clothes were laid out and waiting. We were ready to go. I reclined in bed waiting for the bright green digital display of my clock radio to blink the set time and watched my husband contentedly sleep.

Even though I had gotten virtually no sleep the night before, I was so nervous that all I could do was pace around the house while it seemed my husband was dragging out every moment until our departure. When he asked if I was ready to leave, I snapped back with a flippant answer without meaning to hurt his feelings and quickly apologized for my mood. The journey, some forty minutes to the hospital, included only the road noise and our usual radio station. We were completely lost in our own thoughts. I watched the digital display of the dashboard clock almost obsessively, ticking off the minutes until we arrived. Suddenly I had an awful feeling of doubt about my decision to have the surgery. However, as quickly as the thought entered my mind, a protective stonewall flew up and dashed the notion away.

We arrived on the second floor of the hospital, the surgical center. We were amazed the waiting room was all ready bustling with activity. I signed my name with a shaking hand, as ready as I'd ever be. I sat down, wringing my hands because they felt so naked without my rings, which pre-surgical paperwork instructed be left at home. I heard my name, the nurses so familiar with the pre-surgical protocol a machine could've announced the instructions as effectively.

Get undressed, remove everything, clothes in the bag provided, put on hospital gown, tie in the back, hairnet, and booties, lie down on the gurney and await my return. The preparation procedure was so robotic, I craved some sign of human warmth and comfort. Emotion began to swell and I wiped away tears that threatened to spill over. It felt like my throat was constricting. I really wanted my husband by my side, at least to hold my hand. The nurse stepped in, suddenly embarrassed, I quickly turned aside to conceal my fear. Procedure called for an IV, only a slight pinch or so they said, which in patient terms means to grab the rail and grit your teeth. My husband was escorted in to join me in the cramped little cubical bordered by faded blue curtains, crowded with blinking machines and all manner of medical paraphernalia.

The anesthesiologist popped in, reiterated his instructions from our previous meeting, then detailed the medications he would be giving me. He lost me somewhere around, "I'll be administering..." and I picked up the speech when he said, "...Valium to calm your nerves." That sounded good to me!

As the nurse injected the clear liquid into the IV, I noticed a dizzying effect instantly. My thinking became unclear and I dozed off only to be jarred awake, startled as if I were falling. Had the surgery begun? Was it over? Nope. Finally it was my turn in the surgical suite. I remember being wheeled down the corridor on the gurney as I watched the ceiling tiles quickly pass overhead like a scene in the movie, fascinating. It takes so little to amaze you when you have a sedative.

Now, I was on my way. We reached the end of the corridor and the stretcher halted. We were still just long enough for my husband to peck a kiss on my lips. I desperately wanted to hear "I love you," but he is a man of few words and after more than twenty years together, I know; still...

Whisked through the double doors, you could see wisps of frosty air billow from the freezing room, it was so chilly. The cold, white sterile room had medical gear and lights everywhere. A masked face asked if I was ready. I remember my last thoughts being, "do I really need to answer that?"

Medication flowed into my IV and as it seeped into my veins all thoughts, worries, and anxiety floated away on a cloud. My life was in the hands of the surgeon. I prayed to God to guide his hands.

We had been told the surgery would take approximately one and half-hours. My husband later reported to me that after getting breakfast, he'd returned to the waiting room to await word of my recovery. He appeared to be calmly reading the newspaper but reluctantly admitted his stomach was in knots and the food he'd consumed felt like a rock in his gut. An hour passed, then two. At just over three hours, he began to worry in earnest. No longer able to sit still, desperately wanting a cigarette but afraid to leave the room, he paced the short space between his seat and the window. Finally the doctor sent word there were some complications and we were still in the operating room.

At just over four hours, the doctor appeared. With a serious face, he approached my husband. The surgery had not gone as well as anticipated, though the outcome was not gravely serious. The staple line bisecting the stomach had sprung a leak due to a malfunctioning stapler. The problem led the doctor to put in a double row of staples, which pulled the intestine tighter than what was common. The doctor assured my husband this minor problem was nothing to be concerned about. We'd find out later (and much too late for legal recourse) there was nothing "common" about my surgeon's actions. I would be in recovery for about an hour then sent to a room. He could see me within the hour in recovery. The final prognosis was good and after a moderate recovery period, I would be just fine.

Meanwhile, I awoke in recovery, groggy but feeling very little pain. However, I was not aware of my surroundings until sometime the next day. My husband had made sure to notify everyone on my list I was fine or at least I appeared to be. He reported the complications to no one. After all, there was no need to worry anyone unnecessarily. Appearances can be deceiving and in my case, they were. It would be years later before we would fully discover the extent of the surgeon's obvious deception that day.

Chapter Seven

~ THE FOLLOWING DAYS ~

I opened my eyes, still a little fuzzy the following morning. I was determined to get moving, per the instructions in my gastric by-pass packet concerning a quick recovery. I wanted desperately to do everything just right. A nurse, on one of her routine patient rounds, commented on how well informed and prepared I seemed to be. The compliment felt good.

Then I began to vomit. I was a little concerned but accepted the nausea as a somewhat normal reaction to the surgery according to the literature I had read. My sinuses were draining terribly and thinking that was perhaps the problem, I rang for the nurse and asked for something to help dry them up. My self-diagnosis was confirmed, when I felt the thick mucus drain, I'd instantly gag and throw up. Of course, the nurse would have to consult my surgeon, which she did right away. He suggested a common over the counter sinus medication.

As evening rolled around, I had still been unable to keep down any liquids. The hospital pharmacy had yet to deliver the sinus medication. The nurse, in way of an explanation for my nausea, informed me the drainage was probably filling my little stomach pouch and the liquids I ingested had nowhere to go. Sorry, I know that is a disgusting mental image. The result was that anything I consumed was coming back up. I was receiving IV fluids, pain medication, and something for nausea.

Finally, my husband, against hospital policy, went to a

local store and purchased the sinus medication the doctor had prescribed. The nurse had informed us that it would be at least twenty-four hours before the pharmacy could deliver the meds (even though this was a very common remedy, apparently the hospital pharmacy didn't stock the medication). I continued to sip on the clear liquid diet. Unfortunately, the results were the same. I'd gag and retch. I remained steadfast, determined, failure was not an option. I would be the perfect gastric by-pass patient.

The doctor popped in for a quick visit on the second day after surgery. His perception of my condition was that this experience was quite normal and I should give my body several days to adjust. I tried to remain cheerful. The doctor was very unconcerned, matter of fact, and took his leave in less than three minutes (I timed him). I felt very little reassurance, though I accepted his prognosis without question. After all, he was the expert, right?

I strictly followed the liquid diet. Not because my doctor recommended it, because as yet he hadn't discussed with me what I should or should not consume. I was on a clear liquid diet for the duration of my hospital stay. As the third day dawned, I was sent home. I continued to feel terribly nauseous but I was prepared to deal with the situation on my own. I was noticeably dropping weight but still violently ill every time I attempted to drip any liquid into my newly-formed pouch. I frequently reminded myself of the doctor's words, promising me I would feel better in a few days. I mentally reassured myself with the knowledge I had the strong will of my mother. By sheer force of attitude, I would get through this initial rough patch. I had an appointment for a surgical follow-up in one week. Surely by that point, my condition would have improved.

The following days were very difficult. I continued to follow, to the letter, every detail of my surgery instruction manual. Though my surgeon had offered no post-surgical advice, I remained determined to make all the right moves toward a quick and easy recovery. I felt myself growing weaker rather than gaining strength and this bothered me a great deal.

Breakfast consisted of a can of Ensure (though, I could

only take about two ounces before I felt full then vomited). I tried a little coffee with no sweetener and hot tea, though neither stayed down. I attempted clear broth then later a half of a sugar-free Popsicle. Again and again, I found myself having the same reaction, nausea and vomiting. My husband perused the grocery store aisles for any clear liquids that might appeal to me and that maybe, with some luck, I could tolerate. Unfortunately, nothing seemed to remain in my small pouch for long before I was heaving into an ever-present basin at my side.

My husband tried unsuccessfully to make me as comfortable as possible. He constantly encouraged me to consume something but the resulting nausea and vomiting made me much less inclined. I had no energy, even the short trip to the bathroom from my nearly-permanent station on the couch seemed to sap all the strength I could muster. Exhaustion overwhelmed me and all I wanted to do was sleep. Unconsciousness seemed to be the only relief from the blinding pain that resulted from my frequent bouts of vomiting.

I mentally evaluated everything we were doing. Every teaspoon of "food" going into my mouth strictly adhered to the clear instruction of my information folder to the letter. I felt certain that somehow I was doing something wrong. But what could it be? I put every effort into my recovery; however, now I was beginning to feel very frustrated over my failure. Why did it always come down to a personal failure? Regardless of the reasoning, that was what I felt.

Finally, my one-week appointment came due and we were anxious to have some answers concerning what was going on with me. After the usual preliminaries, the doctor bounded in, his usual flippant self. He began by saying that I should begin adding soft proteins to my diet and walking a minimum of twenty minutes every day to restore my strength. Really, I was astonished!

My concerns went totally unheard and when I questioned him further, the doctor acted as though I were refusing to follow his instructions, scolding me aggressively as if I were a child. He informed me that unless I followed his instructions, the surgery would not be a success and I would never lose weight. I had a desperate problem consuming liquids but was now to add soft proteins and begin walking for exercise when I could scarcely make it from the couch to the bathroom. To avoid a further dressing down, I kept quiet.

The doctor suggested I start with an easy stroll down the driveway and increase a little every day until I was walking at least a half-mile when I returned for my next visit with him in two weeks. I left the office feeling totally dejected and confused. I silently cried all the way home. If I couldn't keep down liquids, how in the world was I to begin eating soft foods? How could I walk when simply changing clothes or going to the bathroom left me completely exhausted? What was I doing wrong? Repeatedly, I asked myself that confrontational question. It never occurred to me at this point that perhaps the surgeon was wrong.

The incision, where the drainage tube entered my abdomen, now appeared to be bright red and angry. When my husband changed the dressing, he noticed a horrible smelling ooze draining from the site. We immediately concluded that the incision was infected. I felt terrible; perhaps the infection was the key to my problems. We called the doctor's office and made an appointment to see him the following morning.

After entering the exam room, he examined my incision and determined that yes it was infected. Of course, an admonishment followed for failure to clean the wound effectively. This was certainly not the case, my husband had cleaned the site very carefully, but there was no arguing with the surgeon.

Using a long Q-tip, the doctor, without warning, jabbed it into the tender wound. I cried out in pain and the look I got could have frozen water into ice. I nearly jumped off the examining table as he began filling the aching space with antibiotic ointment then unceremoniously stuffed gauze wrapping around it. For the most part, the doctor seemed perturbed to see me at all. I still wasn't sure what I had done to earn his displeasure; obviously, I was not his ideal patient.

He suggested that I add peanut butter to my diet and take a B-12 shot to enhance my energy level once a month. I received a stern lecture concerning my lazy attitude toward meeting my walking assignment. Furthermore, unless I followed his instructions to the letter, the surgery would be completely unsuccessful and the responsibility would be on my shoulders alone. We attempted to explain that I remained unable to keep down any sort of sustenance. My husband questioned that perhaps an endoscope might help us find out where the problem might be. The doctor quickly rebuked, and sternly dismissed, any suggestion of testing. He insisted that to do so would do more harm than good at this point. We reluctantly returned home to cope the best way we could.

We tried very hard to follow the doctor's orders. My sweet husband prepared soft scrambled eggs, and brought home sugar-free Jell-O, puréed meats, baby food, carnation instant breakfast and Ensure dietary supplement, to add into my meager diet. Nothing worked. I struggled down the driveway to our mailbox some twenty-five yards, but ended up collapsing near the street and skinning my knees on the asphalt. My husband, who was watching me from the kitchen door, ran to my side. He gently lifted me into his arms and carried me back to the couch. The only progress I made was an unsteady stagger from the couch to the bathroom without falling on my face.

My skin had now taken on a flaky, yellow-tinged pallor. Pain continually contorted my body and nothing seemed to help. After repeatedly calling the doctor, he informed us that he didn't give pain medication for recreational purposes. My face blazed with embarrassment. The surgeon briefly mentioned to my husband that I might be experiencing some psychological problems, rather than anything physical. Frustration had now turned to anguish, then panic, at the mention of the word "psychological."

Someone had to be with me at all times. Sleep remained the only relief from the pain. The doctor had prescribed over-the-counter Benadryl for pain management and sleep. He gave me a prescription for nausea medication that seemed to help somewhat. Any physical action exhausted me, even a short conversation on the phone seemed more than I could deal with at this point. My family and friends called daily to stay abreast of my condition. I became little more than an infant relying on my husband to meet my every need. He took extraordinary care of me. However, we realized something had to change quickly.

By this time, I was nearly comatose. In the short span of three weeks since surgery, I had lost forty pounds. My eyes had sunk into deep, bruised, sunken pools; my skin was flaky and had a sickly yellow pallor; the smell of infection reeked from the wound in my abdomen, even though my husband carefully cleaned and tended to it daily.

I desperately wanted a bath, something more substantial than the gentle sponge off I was getting. It had been three weeks since I had a good cleansing bath. I felt genuinely dirty, gritty, I smelled, and could hardly stand myself. The dried tissue pealed from my arms and legs like a snake shedding its skin. I begged my husband to help me. After considering all of my restrictions, including not wetting any of my incisions, he came up with a solution.

He sterilized the entire bathroom in bleach and hot water. He vigorously cleaned and sterilized a five-gallon bucket then placed it in the tub, using several towels to add padding to the makeshift seat. Because I chilled so easily, he set up an electric heater in the bathroom. Then he carefully washed me with a soft cloth, delicately shaving my underarms and legs; washed my hair, then gently brushed out the thinning strands and towel dried it the best he could. He helped me to brush my teeth. I don't think I have ever loved him more than I did at that moment. It takes quite a man to care for his spouse with the care he has given me. I thank God everyday for him.

When he finished, I was shivering, icy cold, and exhausted. However, I felt clean. This was an enormous relief. He had put clean sheets on our bed and I fell into a debilitated sleep for twelve hours afterward. A simple bath, an afterthought for most people as they start their day or bring an end to their evening, was beyond my capability. Even with enormous assistance, the process had simply kicked my butt.

My husband compiled a table on the computer listing all of my medicines including the amount administered and times each medication was due. He taped the chart to the refrigerator, so that if he was forced to leave my side anyone called in to sit with me knew exactly what to give me and when. He carefully charted everything I ate and when I went to the bathroom.

We had no income, my leave time had now expired and my sweet husband refused to leave me alone; therefore, his business was set aside as well. We began living on credit cards and the kindness of our families. We were only attempting to survive at this point.

I still vomited whenever I tried to eat or drink anything. Finally, the doctor consented to see me in the emergency room. He ordered an upper GI series then armed with the results and waving them like a banner, he declared I had no physical problems, thus no reason to complain. Therefore, he concluded the pain, nausea, and vomiting were undoubtedly psychotic in origin. My husband was furious. Barely conscious, I was too weak to react at all.

Chapter Eight

~ *THE ROCKY PATH OF RECOVERY* ~

I continued to stagger down the path to recovery; however, we had discovered minefields along the way. Unfortunately, this segment of my journey comes from copious notes compiled by my husband. He kept a detailed diary of the days, weeks, months, and years to follow. I have very little memory of the next two years of my life and months after that are spotty. Fleeting remembrances involve writhing in bed, suffering from excruciating pain or feeling my senses chemically dulled as I succumbed to the oblivion of medication.

I was barely coherent. My body still maintained "life" but the existence of my body was far from actually living. Imagine waking from a coma only to realize that time had passed you by. The reality is terrifying.

Seasons have come and gone; my children have grown and changed, life has progressed for everyone except me. No matter how much I read and studied, no matter how meticulously I prepared for coping with every aspect of gastric bypass surgery and living; this horrible outcome was impossible to anticipate. Never in my wildest nightmares had I seen myself in the depths of hell that was my life since the surgery. The surgeon remained completely unconcerned and continued to insist that I was psychologically impaired.

I was then eight weeks out of surgery; still there was no relief in sight. Family and friends were terrified that death would soon take me. The situation was grave (the pun is definitely intended). Our professional and private lives were in shambles. We no longer prayed for good health, we prayed for just one more day.

My husband could no longer stand the sight of my suffering. He resolved to take me to the hospital emergency room and refuse to leave until my condition stabilized. Our arrival only added to a room already filled to capacity with afflicted humanity. Of course, who else would be there? Unless a patient passed out, bled on the floor or threw up everywhere, each individual waited his or her turn. My pain was unbearable. I paced, I cried, I curled up into a tight fetal position in a hard plastic chair, and then I paced some more. There was no comforting me. All the while, I discreetly threw up in a small hospital basin. I tried very hard to maintain some semblance of composure in public … old habits die-hard even when I was out of my mind with pain.

The surgeon was not on call this particular night so his partner stepped in to fill the void. This doctor was the polar opposite of my original surgeon. He expressed thoughtful concern and his sole purpose was to relieve my pain as quickly as possible. His bedside manner, caring concern, and immediate treatment brought tears of relief to my eyes. This physician was everything my own doctor was not. The only fault I could find with this doctor was his judgment at choosing a medical partner that was lacking in bedside manner or common patient care. (I use the past tense but the two doctors are still partners as of this writing.)

I was extremely dehydrated and losing weight far too rapidly. More than a pound a day evaporated from my ever-shrinking frame. The on-call physician admitted me to the surgical floor immediately and there I stayed for the following ten days. My own doctor popped his head in the door next morning, somewhat cheerfully. We had no idea what he had to be so pleased with; we were not in on the joke.

True to form, he blamed the entire episode on me. He informed us that because I refused to follow doctor's orders, I would continually be sick. The doctor advised that I should force myself to consume at least a full gallon of water per day. I repeatedly attempted to explain that whenever I tried to drink or eat anything, no matter what it was or the consistency of it,

I immediately threw up. The doctor looked at me with apparent disgust and stated he had no time for my "excuses." With a wave of dismissal, he left the room, motioning for my husband to follow. He took my husband aside to explain that I displayed symptoms of severe mental illness to the point that I had chosen to live in this dilapidated state in order to garner attention. The doctor determined I should be admitted to the psychiatric floor or perhaps a psychiatric treatment facility. He suspected I was schizophrenic and would most likely benefit from rigorous anti-psychotic drugs.

My wonderful husband was so angry, he had to walk away from the man who called himself a health care professional. This doctor was virtually condemning me to death. Later his partner, who had admitted me, stopped in to check on my progress and innocently asked what tests would be run. I could only shake my head negatively, with tears rolling down my cheeks. He was obviously dismayed but didn't dare intervene—after all I was not his patient. When we inquired about changing surgeons within the practice, we were quickly informed the physicians had an agreement that except for a case of on-call or emergency situations, they would not transfer patients among themselves. Should a patient desire a second opinion, the patient would have to go outside their practice.

I remained in the hospital connected to a constant drip of Dilaudid. The drug is one of the most powerful pain medications available; terminally ill patients often receive this medication for pain. Still, during brief lucid moments, violent heaves shuddered through my body and I literally trembled in pain. Then my body drifted from consciousness to oblivion. Abruptly, some ten days after my admission into the hospital, a nurse strolled in, unhooked the IV and informed us I was being released. No explanation, no change in my condition, other than a few hours of drug-induced peace to relieve the daily torturous nightmare my life had become. The continuous pump of IV fluid had only bloated my malnourished body. The temporary water weight gained was literally flushed away within a few days.

Within the first twelve hours of darkening our door, I was

very close to delirium. Heart-wrenching sobs and uncontrollable convulsions pushed me over an imaginable edge. My shrieks reached our neighbors who came running to our aid.

My husband placed a frantic call to the surgeon whose response was the same diatribe we'd come to expect. His prejudicial diagnosis was that I had obviously continued to deteriorate mentally. The surgeon suggested that since the constant attention of the hospital staff was withdrawn, I was acting out to be noticed. Further, the doctor felt my husband's denial to recognize this condition enabled me to continue my delusional behavior. My husband completely disregarded the admonishment, refusing to accept the berating personal judgment.

Without so much as acknowledging the doctor's statement, my husband suggested to the doctor that perhaps my adverse reaction might be due to the sudden withdrawal from the intensive pain medication. He was shocked when the surgeon rebuked the suggestion, stating that I had not been prescribed pain medication. The surgeon abruptly ended the conversation. With no further explanation or advice, he hung up the phone. My husband was holding the receiver and listening to dead air. The surgeon had no concern, and certainly no relief, for my already fragile situation. We were left to fend for ourselves once again, nowhere to turn.

Why didn't we seek out a second opinion at this point? The answer is hardly simple. We honestly accepted my surgeon's explanation as the authority. We are of an age that respects authority figures and at that point we were trying to adhere to all of his directions. At every turn he offered us a small semblance of hope and we clung to it, like a life raft while adrift at sea.

Later, we discovered that the truth of the matter was, in fact, his associate had prescribed the pain medication on the day of admission to the hospital. The notation to that fact was there in my hospital medical chart. We concluded, because of my surgeon's reaction, that he'd never consulted my chart to glean my onset diagnosis or treatment administered by his partner when I was brought into the emergency room. Preconceived notions, drug interactions, or contrary treatment could easily have killed me simply due to the surgeon's refusal to read my chart.

For two days, my husband lovingly held me while I cried. He soothed me, rocking me as if I were an infant. He wanted only to calm me, drying unexplained tears. We prayed that the reaction was only some sort of withdrawal from the pain medication and would soon pass. Just when I began to doubt my own sanity, I fell into a restless slumber. When I woke, my emotions were under better control.

We experienced this same reaction many times. Largely due to my husband's self-taught medical skills, we were able to recognize the situation for what it truly was: drug withdrawal. Realization didn't make the uncontrolled emotional outbursts any easier to deal with. To avoid this terrible ordeal, the doctor could've simply ordered a slow weaning process off the extremely potent pain medications like morphine and Dilaudid that so often coursed through my veins.

By this time, we'd grown somewhat accustomed to the doctor's medical indifference that we continued to accept his behavior. We eventually came to the fearful realization that trust must be earned and this surgeon was not to be trusted. We began to actively search for another doctor to see me. It didn't take long to realize how difficult it would be to find a physician willing to step in when a doctor and patient clash.

By now I had dropped some sixty pounds. Our local hospital and her sister hospital forty miles to the north where I'd had my surgery were all too familiar haunts now. We spent nearly as much time there as in our own home. Over the next two years, I never spent more than fifteen consecutive days at home before the next admission into one of these hospitals. We knew the staff by first name and they knew my history so well, the check-in procedures were nearly robotic without our ever saying a word. Of course, hospital regulations would never allow that.

I had blood work drawn weekly; however, the results were not available to us. We continued to plead with the doctor to perform an endoscope, but he steadfastly refused. By the middle of May 2002, spring had arrived, which always seems to reinvigorate me. My editors were hard at work on the final checks of my first book. We were hoping for a Christmas release date. I was a very green author then. My medical situation continued to prohibit the book's introduction onto the market. Work on my first book had come to a complete standstill. I was unable to do my part toward its release; therefore, I was obliged to turn over the entire project to my editor. To give her a well-deserved pat on the back, without her constant encouragement and downright badgering, my first book would never have become a reality. I hated the situation but had no choice at this point.

Weakness, fatigue, pain, and vomiting were the pasttimes that consumed my daily schedule. Day to day living remained torturous and frustrating. I sank into a deep dark depression. I continued a pattern of physical deterioration a little more each day. It was alarming to my family and friends as they watched my decline and tragically feared for my life. Helplessly there seemed to be little anyone could do to stop the plunging downward spiral.

June arrived and I found myself in the hospital suffering from dehydration once again. Unfortunately, this was a terrible time in my life to find myself incarcerated in my medical confines. I awoke on a sunny summer morning, but my sad demeanor remained despite the glorious day. It was my landmark fortieth birthday. I "celebrated" my birthday unceremoniously and virtually alone in the hospital. Life was passing me by. I remained in the unrelenting grips of pain and despair.

The date has always been especially dear to me because I share the birthday with our oldest son. Traditionally, we have always shared the day together but this year he celebrated alone. While most celebrate or mourn this day as an official triumph to middle age, I just prayed that I would live beyond the year, this month, the week, or see the sunlight dawning on the next clear summer's day. My tremendous support group did their best to cheer me but I was inconsolable. I was imprisoned within the confines of a sterile hospital room. Depressed and weak as a newborn, Happy Birthday to me!

Amazingly, by July I felt well enough to return to work part-time. I was able to keep down a little yogurt but still no solid foods. For three glorious days, I returned to my "real" job. Then on Thursday morning, I began to feel intense pain.

This was a pain that I had yet to experience, gripping my lower back then fanning across my right side, my appendix, I thought. I stepped into my supervisor's office to let him know I needed to leave. Without my uttering a word, he asked if I needed an ambulance. Pain contorted my face like a grotesque mask.

I declined the ambulance, leaving work and heading home on my own (brave or stupid?). When I reached the main road, it was obvious I was going to change course and go straight to the emergency room. I called my husband on the way and asked him to meet me there. Very slowly and carefully, I drove the scant two miles to the hospital at no more than thirty miles an hour, all the while thanking God the hospital was so close. I parked and as I stepped out of the car, I collapsed in a heap to the sizzling parking lot pavement. Stunned but with great effort, I dragged myself to my feet then stumbled toward the emergency room door. I stumbled again and when I collapsed this time, all energy drained from me there on the burning asphalt drive. I was terrified. I heard people gathering around me in alarm but I couldn't distinguish any voice or clearly define the slow motion figures moving around me. The tormenting throes of pain were very near unbearable as nausea rose up in my throat. I gagged but only produced thick yellow bile spewing from my cramping abdomen.

Luckily, the emergency room was empty. The registration nurse didn't even attempt to question me, only taking my purse to obtain identification. The triage doctor attempted to help me onto the examination table when I slipped to the floor in a dead faint. He lifted me in his arms and settled me onto the gurney. Barely conscious, in a halting voice, I tried desperately to describe my condition as well as my complicated medical history while I faded in and out of oblivion.

I was immediately hooked to an IV and Demerol administered. The pain refused to subside. After consulting my surgeon, the emergency room staff determined that I should be transferred to the larger hospital forty miles to the north. Gratefully, drugs made the trip as painless as possible. My husband arrived as the ambulance pulled up to take me away. He frantically exceeded all speed limits with emergency flashers blinking in tune with his rapid heartbeat following close behind the ambulance.

I was pale, fading in and out of consciousness, blissfully unaware of anything going on around me. I don't remember anything about the check-in process at the hospital, so undoubtedly everything went forward without a hitch. The overall plan, as explained to us, was to relieve my pain and conduct some diagnostic testing. We felt this was a huge step forward. I had enough pain anesthetizing medication to tranquilize an elephant.

The next morning my doctor whisked into the room obviously very pleased. He stated that he'd discovered the cause of all of my problems. The source of all my problems appeared to be a fistula. Simply put, a fistula is a leak in the stomach wall. Though this is not a common problem, it wasn't an unheard of complication for gastric by-pass patients. We felt vindicated and relieved to finally have a diagnosis for the torture I had endured.

The treatment for this condition involved avoiding all stress to the stomach lining. In other words, for the next six-weeks, I'd be fed intravenously. In order to begin, the doctor would place a central line in the carotid artery. When I heard these words, terror gripped my chest. The line would provide all of my nutrition to allow the fistula time to heal. The problem should heal on its own during this period. I could take in nothing by mouth except tiny slivers of ice for the duration of the treatment. The orders weren't hard to follow, especially since ingesting food of any sort made me sick.

Without further ado, the doctor set about inserting the line right there at my hospital bed. A sharp pain seared through my neck as the fat needle pierced my skin, and then the intense pressure seized my entire right side as the line snaked along its course. I had never been so scared in my life but the doctor ignored my emotions as tears silently slid down my cheeks and my body trembled.

Instructions during the hospital dismissal process the next morning held a big surprise. The orders stated that a home healthcare nurse would visit us on three occasions to teach my husband how to care for me with the new central line. He'd be required to administer total parenteral nutrition, commonly called TPN. The treatment is simply a vehicle to feed intravenously when a patient is unable to take nourishment conventionally, circumventing the stomach. Immediately following each feeding, the lines must be flushed with heparin then saline and the process repeated twice daily for six weeks.

From the start, flushing the ports resulted in a metallic taste in my mouth. The sensation would automatically trigger intense nausea leading to powerful gagging then vomiting which contorted my entire body in severe pain. We handled this in the usual fashion that had become so familiar, pain medication leading to oblivious unconsciousness.

About three days into the treatment while attempting to access the port leading to the central line, my husband met with some sort of blockage. Afraid to force the issue, he notified the attending nurse who responded immediately. She actually lived in our neighborhood and was at our door within minutes. Working with the line, she managed to get it cleared. However, she was very uncomfortable about the way the process was working so decided to stay and observe the entire feeding. Once the TPN had finished, she watched closely to ensure my husband was following through correctly. She noted that his technique was perfect.

Although he had reported the violent reaction I had to the line flush and had kept a record of each instance, it seemed no one really grasped the extent of this reaction. The nurse was shocked when my temperature and blood pressure soared, my heart began to race threatening tachycardia, and then my body went into soul-wracking dry heaves. The nurse immediately took over my care and put a stop to the treatment. She called for an ambulance and without ever leaving my side, placed a call to my doctor.

The sirens blasted as the ambulance pulled into our driveway and EMT's rushed into our bedroom. The doctor still hadn't returned the call, even though the answering service had said he'd receive the emergency message within five minutes. The nurse rode with me to the hospital as my husband followed behind. She gave her detailed report to the triage doctor, assuring him my doctor was aware of the situation.

She left us in the very capable hands of the emergency room staff. My doctor left a message for the emergency room staff to stabilize my condition and send me home. The staff had no choice but to follow the doctor's orders.

The next day while administering the TPN, my husband met with the same results as the previous day. He refused to continue the treatment. He just could not inflict this torture any longer. We had no idea what to do or who to turn to. He called the nurse who assured us she'd speak to the doctor directly. Twenty-four hours later, we still hadn't heard anything from the doctor. We contacted our home health care nurse again and she attempted to contact the doctor once again to no avail. Understandably, I began to suffer from great bouts of anxiety, depression, crying, inability to sleep, nervousness along with the usual pain, nausea, and vomiting. Finally, now that the doctor had his diagnosis, my mental faculties had truly begun to deteriorate.

My husband had an appointment with our family doctor for his yearly physical. He arranged for a friend to sit with me and left to see the doctor. When she simply asked about me, he very uncharacteristically broke down. She was stunned. This reaction was so out of character for him. Suddenly the entire vivid story came pouring out and he couldn't stop crying. The doctor prescribed some antidepressants for him (although he never took more than one or two of them). She calmed him and asked if he would bring me in to see her.

At this point, I was so weak it took two people just to move me. A friend carried my intravenous fluid paraphernalia while my husband carried me. I could only manage a few steps on my own now. I had lost over seventy pounds in approximately four months. We were a sorry looking trio as we entered her examination room. Waiting patients visibly gasped and stared as we made our way through the outer office, but I was oblivious. The staff found a room for me, trying to make me as comfortable as possible. I was in and out of consciousness. She'd been our family doctor for over ten years and could not conceal the horror on her face. She immediately went into action. She prescribed a durogesic pain patch in an effort to stabilize my pain and begged us to get another opinion. She recommended a doctor just south of us. She pulled my husband aside, saying that she feared for my life and pleaded with him to get help for me immediately. She sincerely felt I'd be dead within thirty days. Sadly, we discounted her advice as somewhat biased because she had so vehemently opposed the surgery to begin with. This was our fault entirely, our doctor really tried.

Unfortunately, soon after this appointment, for personal reasons, our family doctor closed her practice. Like all of the patients in her care, we were transferred to another primary care physician who assumed her patients. After reading my chart, he refused to see me. He claimed, understandably so, that my health problems were too extensive for him to handle. The only care we expected was the very basic medical attention, unfortunately, when one small problem cropped up, it quickly escalated into a much more serious complication. Even sinus drainage, very common for our area, would result in my being unable to hold down even a mere sip of water. The resulting dehydration usually led to yet another hospital stay.

Eventually, another local doctor agreed to take me on with the understanding that serious problems concerning my surgery would be dealt with by my gastrointestinal surgeon. The situation didn't quite end up that way, much to this physician's chagrin. He ended up doing countless hours of research and study on ministering to me. He cared for me as well as he possibly could, not having ever dealt with anyone in my situation. There were times when we'd cry together because neither of us knew how to deal with the numerous complications I continually faced.

It was at this point that an incredible nurse came into my life. She wasn't the only nurse who cared for me who was absolutely a God's send. There were, and continue to be, some very wonderful nurses and technicians who have come into my life. But this particular nurse literally saved my life on more than one occasion. I thank her sincerely. Many of the visiting nurses continue to this day to be very dear friends. I could never explain how deeply we appreciate their expert care and truly unlimited kindness. Thank you is such a little thing; you all are my angels.

My husband was irate by this time and was determined to force the surgeon to act. He stubbornly placed another call to him. My primary visiting nurse was appalled at the doctor's failure to respond. She, in fact, notified the state medical board who never took any action. (That is our tax dollars at work.) Finally, after three very long days, he returned the call. My husband went into detail, explaining the latest situation well-documented by my home health care nurse.

Paying no heed, the doctor insisted I was yet again plagued with mental problems. He further stated it was simply impossible to have this kind of reaction to the heparin or saline when administered via the central line. We had no recourse except to continue the prescribed treatment. With a heavy heart, we pressed on.

For four additional days, my husband put me through hell every time he flushed the line; at this point, he completely discontinued all TPN treatments. He called the surgeon again. The two men actually began screaming at each other over the phone. My husband was frantic with worry over me and the surgeon angrily refused to admit me into the hospital unless my husband would agree to have me committed to the psychiatric ward for evaluation. The surgeon vehemently continued his argument there was positively nothing physically wrong with me. His diagnosis remained psychotic delusions, schizophrenia, and an inability to mentally deal with the gastric bypass surgery.

Finally, after a very heated quarrel, the two men came to an amicable compromise. I was privy to none of this information. The doctor agreed to admit me to the hospital on the surgical floor for testing purposes, if my husband agreed to allow the staff psychologist to evaluate me. Unfortunately, when we arrived the doctor stated he did not intend to conduct any tests, firmly believing all of my complications lay within the confines of my own mind. He refused to hold up his end of bargain. However, at least I was now under constant, trained medical supervision once again.

The psychologist came in within an hour of my hospital admission; obviously, the surgeon had notified her prior to my arrival and was wasting no time. He was convinced he could influence my husband and have me locked away in a psychiatric ward if the psychologist would back up his diagnosis.

The psychologist asked if she could speak to me alone and I agreed as long as my husband was not too far away. After assuring me that he would be right outside the door, he stepped out of the room. She casually inquired about my life, my family, and my medical history. Then she delved into the situation since my surgery. True to my character, my life is an open book; I explained my medical situation in as much detail as possible. After approximately an hour, she seemed to have all of the information she required and asked if I would agree to take an anti-depressant. After asking some questions about the medication, I assented.

We never received her evaluation, but over a year later, when we obtained my medical records her conclusions were included in my files. It was her opinion that I was experiencing normal anxieties associated with the stress of my medical complications. She felt that anyone having undergone what I had been through following surgery would be inclined to react the same way. It made us feel better that at least we were somewhat vindicated if only in a small way.

I was so distressed that I was terrified to be alone. It was extremely paranoid of me but I felt threatened. Today, I feel this was nothing less than extreme mental abuse on the surgeon's part. Against my wishes, my husband left me alone in the hospital overnight. I cried pitifully when he left me. We had no way of knowing what was about to happen. A new era in this saga was about to begin.

I was stunned when I opened my eyes the next morning and the surgeon stood beside my hospital bed. It was seven o'clock and he informed me I'd be going into surgery within the hour. I was in shock. He intended to do an exploratory endoscope and to insert a feeding tube. I could barely speak, before I could ask any questions and with no further explanation, the doctor left the room.

I would be going into surgery within the hour and my husband was more than forty miles away. I frantically dialed our home number and waited as the ringing phone summoned him. He was skeptical; the doctor had previously insisted he would do no testing, now without any reasoning or explanation, I was going into surgery. We had begged that he do the endoscope for months. What spurred this change of heart, we would never know.

I was taken into pre-op alone and afraid. Luckily, one of my cousins, who I vaguely knew, worked in pre-op and she helped calm me. Literally, moments before they wheeled me into the surgical suite, my husband came rushing through the double doors leading to the holding area. My sister, who had arrived the night before from more than three hours away, was right on his heels. Deeply concerned at what new complication had led to this action, my husband, sister, and youngest son, waited patiently to speak to the doctor. He refused to see them prior to the procedures.

I'm not exactly sure how long the procedure lasted. During the exploratory, my esophagus was actually strictured, completely closed off with scar tissue. Another surgeon was called in for emergency treatment to dilate the esophageal opening to allow food, liquid, or medication to pass through. I would have to endure six additional dilation procedures every two weeks to keep my esophagus open.

The surgeon met with my family once I was sent to recovery. He actually apologized for his misdiagnosis and admitted he'd made some terrible mistakes (those were his words). He actually appeared to be contrite. He finally agreed he should've performed the endoscope much sooner.

A feeding tube or rather a Foley catheter, generally used for kidney catheterization, was implanted into my abdomen to allow some sort of nutrition. He removed the central line but I was to remain on a clear liquid diet indefinitely. We finally had a diagnosis of esophageal stricture, dehydration, and malnutrition.

The fistula had never existed at all. The hell we had endured throughout the time with the central line had been unnecessary torture. The fistula turned out to be a shadow on the X-ray. I left the hospital three days later. Unfortunately, there were few signs of improvement. However, we now had hope and prayed for a new diagnosis. We finally felt that we had something to work with. Progress, but for how long would this false sense of security last? Not long.

Chapter 9

~ CARRYING ON ~

One week later, we sat in the surgeon's examination room when he entered looking embarrassed. I was shocked when his first words to me were, "for what it's worth, I'm sorry." Sorry for what, I wondered. The misdiagnosis, the neglect, his uncaring bedside manner, and/or his mental abuse; he had a number of things to be sorry for. I was just relieved to have a diagnosis. I felt better knowing we were moving in the right direction. I was willing to put most of my apprehension aside. However, my psyche would never be the same and I no longer had any faith in my surgeon. Even today, I bear irreparable scars from his continual threats as well as his insistence that I belonged in a psychiatric ward.

I remain terrified, to this day, scarred by the surgeon's continual threats, and further of the stigma associated with a mentally deficient diagnosis. The thought of losing control of my mental faculties is not a situation that I can imagine. Intellectually, I realize that today we live in a different age where psychiatric therapy is no longer a character flaw; in fact, today it is quite in vogue. Four out of every ten people take some form of anti-depressants, according to the American Medical Association. However irrational this thought process might be, for me, I cannot accept an emotionally unstable diagnosis. On the other hand, I do not see counseling as some awful flaw in other people. The mentally ill stigma is simply something I was taught from an early age as an incredible weakness.

During my next medical appointment, after explaining

my continued nausea and vomiting, the doctor suggested that in many cases it took thirteen weeks before gastric by-pass patients actually recover sufficiently from the surgery. He explained that often, suddenly after this period the patient will feel better, begin to eat without problem and regain their strength. We laughingly began to refer to this as the "magical thirteenth week theory." We did not really accept this rationale as a realistic explanation of my condition. Still, we continued to follow the doctor's advice, naively relying on his "expertise." We remained respectful of the surgeon, desperate to believe he had my best interest at heart.

I complained to the doctor that I continued to feel intense pain in my lower abdomen and experienced a great deal of nausea after I had consumed anything, be it liquid or soft solid. He informed me he'd already prescribed one of the most potent nausea medications available by prescription, which was Compazine. We countered that he hadn't given me this medication with the exception of my repeated hospital stays. He consulted my medical chart, which supported our claim. Even though the chart clearly noted all of my prescribed medications, the surgeon continued to argue, concluding I was perhaps abusing prescription medications. This was not the first time he'd confused my prescriptions. On several occasions, my chart in hand, the surgeon prescribed medications that I had previous allergic reactions to.

In fact, the surgeon constantly tried to treat me with Phenergan, the most popular drug for nausea and vomiting. We repeatedly reiterated to him I was allergic to this medication. In the hospital at one point, a Phenergan shot resulted in my entire body contorting into severe muscle spasms, hives, itching, and a feeling of burning in my hands and feet.

The reaction was not life threatening, however, the attending nurse instructed us to inform any medical professional treating me in the future that I was allergic to this medication. She noted the reaction in my chart with a large red stripe across the front stating "Phenergan allergy." The nurse stated that other common medications could be utilized to accomplish the same result. In her opinion, there was no reason to subject me to possibly severe complications. The surgeon, in a very matter-of-fact manner, lectured us that it was impossible to have an allergic reaction to Phenergan. In his estimation, my experience with this drug interaction was purely psychological. I could not believe we were back to this same sermon. Here we go again, now my allergic reactions to certain drugs were psychotic. The doctor was obviously determined to hang a psychological diagnosis on me.

I began to wonder if the surgeon wouldn't be satisfied until I was irreparably damaged or dead. What had I done to deserve this sort of treatment? We felt his treatment was beginning to reek of pure negligence. He concluded this visit by suggesting that perhaps I was experiencing gas pains then suggested I use an over the counter laxative to relieve the intestinal pressure.

Over the next week, I was to undergo the second dilation procedure in the capable hands of the specialist who had performed the previous procedure. Gratefully, I had sedation for the dilation—it was an outpatient operation. The pain afterward was not unbearable but certainly uncomfortable. The procedure resulted in my returning to nothing but clear liquids, which for me meant my old standard, chicken and stars soup. The familiar product had been my constant source of sustenance since the surgery. At this point, the majority of gastric by-pass patients would be eating small amounts of a regular diet. In my case, if it was a good day, I was fortunate to keep down clear chicken broth. I was very discouraged.

We no longer dealt with the horrible complications day-by-day but moment-to-moment. My condition often plunged to a crisis within minutes. Within days of the dilation procedure, my husband had no choice but to rush me to our local hospital emergency room, suffering with severe pain, unable to go to the bathroom. X-rays confirmed an intestinal obstruction and impaction. The emergency room physician and nurses tried for the better part of the day with laxatives, mineral oil, soap enemas, as well as manual removal of the blockage. A fecal impaction is a large mass of dry, hard stool that can develop in the rectum due to chronic constipation. Impaction is common in cases such as mine resulting from the lack of sufficient hydration, pain medications, anti-diarrhea medications, as well as limited mobility.

The emergency room staff tried for endless hours to relieve me, unfortunately nothing seemed to work. As a last ditch effort I found myself admitted. A gastrointestinal specialist came to my aid; the examination revealed that surgery was a distinct possibility if the blockage was not resolved within the next twenty-four hours. Our family physician tried to remove the blockage manually but my bowels held numerous rock solid masses. I had excruciating intestinal cramping as my body instinctively tried to expel the foreign matter. To complicate matters in what had become common for my condition, I remained severely dehydrated. I had strained so much I had begun to bleed from the rectum. Unfortunately, because pain medication slows down the intestinal process, nothing could be given to alleviate the horrible spasms.

The specialist attempted one final maneuver to force the offending waste from my system. An aggressive laxative, some special concoction mixed by the gastroenterologist, gratefully the mixture went by way of the feeding tube. The doctor counseled should this option fail, the only alternative left would be surgery. Fortunately, within the hour, the laxative worked. No one can imagine the relief I felt when the huge clots were cleansed from my body. The engorging pain was much less intense, yet my body still ached from the constant strain to relieve myself. Physically, exhaustion ebbed through my entire body and gave way to rejuvenating sleep.

Unfortunately, the impaction caused both internal and external bleeding hemorrhoids. At first, the doctor tried medication but the bleeding became very profuse so he recommended surgery. The gastrointestinal doctor removed the hemorrhoid using a laser under general anesthesia. The whole process was over in a matter of minutes and all that remained was a tender bottom for several days afterward.

The specialist determined that a colonoscopy was necessary before surgery in order to examine my bowels for further abscesses or ulcers. Within the hour, I was in the procedure room, a heart monitor taped around my finger and several places on my chest and back as well. As the monitor began to beep in rhythm with my heart, an image of mother's death flashed through my mind. The horrible last vigil as we help-lessly stared at the monitor in a steady decline to zero, then watching as her heartbeat registered for the last time. I sud-denly found it hard to breathe. I was moaning then sobbing uncontrollably. A fierce panic attack seized my body. I could not speak and no one in the room could identify the problem.

The nurse went for my husband who came in to calm me then valium finished the job. Finally, I was calm enough to explain through dreadful cries. My husband held me until the medication chemically stilled my terror. The doctor was now able to begin the procedure, within an hour it was over and I was awake again. I said a prayer of thanks to God and Mama.

Our new family doctor had written orders that my feeding tube site should be cleaned daily. While following this instruc-tion, the attending nurse inadvertently cut the stitches securing the Foley catheter. I wasn't aware of the situation or the dan-ger of this snafu. At first there had been approximately four inches of this tube outside my body, however by the next morning the entire tube with the exception of the Y-connector had disappeared into the abyss of my abdomen.

Once my husband arrived, I had him look at the feeding tube. He quickly concluded this situation could not be good. We called the nurse and asked if, in their opinion, this might cause further problems. She assured us this was perfectly normal. The next morning I was sent home, still throwing up and only able to consume clear liquids. I had now shed more than eighty-five pounds.

The next week involved doctors' appointments and pro-cedures. I had my third dilation then the next day an upper GI was scheduled. When you identify the floor nurses, radiology staff, operating room nurses, and outpatient surgery staff by their first names, you realize you've become a fixture in the hospital. I had gotten to know these people so well I began asking about their husbands, wives and kids by name as well. My husband knew the cafeteria personnel by name.

The radiologist reported there was no clearly defined ob-struction resulting in my ever-increasing pain. For the first time, another amazing revelation was made. The radiologist report stated, "The gastric pouch could not be clearly identified," meaning, they could not find a gastric pouch or stomach, even when utilizing a highly reliable dye test. Our family doctor was very concerned at this point and felt the Foley catheter was the main source of my pain. He repeatedly questioned us and eventually called my surgeon concerning how long the catheter would remain.

By the following Monday morning, I was in such excruciating pain I could not walk or even stand. My husband called, literally begging the surgeon to see me. I had completely collapsed, huddled tightly in a fetal position. The doctor, grudgingly, agreed to work me into his busy schedule that afternoon.

The nurse who did the preliminary vital signs was very concerned when she was unable to get a blood pressure reading. She tried many times, using several different blood pressure cuffs and calling other nurses to have a go at it. Still nothing registered; it was as if I were dead. My complexion was sallow; I was feverish and had no more strength than a newborn. She alerted the surgeon in a panic that he should examine me immediately and perhaps summon an ambulance. When he entered the room, the surgeon noted that I "looked terrible." I agreed. While the nurse waited anxiously, ready to call for an ambulance, he dismissed her with a wave of his hand then closed the door in her face.

Granted, the sole purpose of this surgery was to lose weight but I was obviously starving to death, which was never my intent. When the doctor came in exhibiting his usual flippant attitude, we questioned him concerning the placement of my feeding tube. He didn't feel the placement was a problem but to satisfy us he would check. Well, thank you for small favors!

He left the room, returning a moment later with a syringe. The doctor deflated the balloon securing the tube, sliding it out a few inches then refilled it. My husband noted it was as if my pain was instantly relieved, the color returned to my face and suddenly I felt near complete relief from the most intense pain.

The consensus was that a nurse had obviously cut the stitch holding the catheter in place. The natural peristalsis (movement of digestion in the intestine) had pulled the feeding tube bulb into my intestinal tract causing a Vasa vacuum. In layman's terms, this meant that my intestinal tract had been blocked for approximately two weeks. If the situation had continued, I would have died a slow, painful death. Very pleased with himself for resolving this dilemma, the surgeon repeated his oft-mentioned mantra of the "magical thirteen weeks." In unison, we rolled our eyes in disbelief.

After the doctor had left the room, the same nurse who had taken my vital signs stepped into the room and shut the door. Taken completely off guard, we listened as she began telling us about the problems involving the surgeon with his staff and patients. Recently his staff, as a whole, had brought him to task. The staff identified many problems concerning his behavior, including his non-existent beside manner, as well as his handling of patients and staff with a cold and brusque attitude.

Further, the staff felt his constant failure to listen, or completely disregard the complaints of his patients, was unacceptable. According to this nurse, his response was that if anyone, including his patients or staff, was dissatisfied with him, they were free to leave immediately. Obviously, the staff had wasted their breath on this man. He did not intend to change his attitudes to accommodate anyone.

As the nurse left the room, my husband and I looked at each other in complete shock. Why was she sharing this information with us? The nurse astounded us by saying she was aware of "mistakes" made in my case and was very sorry I was going through the extensive complications. She assured us I was not the only patient suffering from the incredible complications, but of course, stopped short of naming any other patient. The nurse insisted the complications, with proper treatment, might have been completely avoided. We stared at each other in stunned silence. As we made our way home, we wondered why this nurse chose to work for a doctor she knew to be guilty of medical malpractice. Why did she share this information with us?

Five days later the surgeon removed the Foley catheter and replaced it with a proper feeding tube. He insisted I must consume as much protein as possible, specifically noting refried beans as an excellent source. The surgeon vehemently reiterated it was imperative that I walk at least a half-mile each day. Although I didn't argue with him at this point, we found his directions ridiculous and impossible to follow, given my present state.

We explained to him I was still unable to keep down liquids and continued to suffer excruciating gas pains. The pain repeatedly gripped my abdomen and chest so intensely, I feared I might have a heart attack ... refried beans could only exacerbate this situation. Suggesting I should walk a half-mile per day was ludicrous. I was barely able to walk from the bed to the bathroom, some ten feet. My husband continued to assist me in bathing because I was so weak, even something as simple as taking care of my own hygiene needs was nearly impossible. How could this man look at me and suggest these things? It was clear that my health remained tenuous.

July 2002 was a tough month for me. In the midst of my dismal recovery, the day had finally come for my sister to go into surgery. I was terrified for her. Sleep would not come as I envisioned all the possibilities of gastric by-pass surgery that were now all too familiar to me. My concern for her far overshadowed my well-being. She was mentally ready for the surgery but I felt a deep sense of guilt for many reasons. Foremost, I was simply too ill to be there for her as she had been for me. I desperately wanted to be by her side. As a witness to my predicament, my sister knew firsthand the possible problems she might face, which only added to her natural anxiety concerning the surgery. She never complained. My sister is so dear to me that the thought of her going through the agony I had experienced was virtually impossible for me imagine. I recalled suffering with her at the birth of her children and this was so much more serious.

Because she had more weight to contend with, I knew her process would be more difficult. Without a doubt, she faced the situation bravely. I prayed this surgery was the answer to a life long struggle for her and she'd avoid the worst of these complications. The two of us have shared the best of times and the worst of times, it was only natural that we would share this as well.

Much to my relief, she came through the surgery with no problems at all. I still worried as she faced recovery and continually prayed for her. I would gratefully handle all the complications as long as she avoided them. Because I am more than eight years older, I realize now that I felt a motherly concern. The thought of my sister in pain was frightening. I tried to be careful not to add to her anxiety. I kept a lot of the negativity I felt for the surgery to myself as we spoke to one another during daily chats.

Regardless of how well my sister's gastric by-pass surgery turned out, I knew with certainty she was facing the same vomiting, gas pains and assorted other common occurrences after the procedure. We continually shared "war stories." I truly believe that going through this common experience has brought us closer than we have ever been in the past. Growing up, we were separated by so many years, we had little in common, but now as adults I continue to love her as a sister yet now I value her as a dear friend. Her support has been unwavering and I desperately wanted give her the full support she had so lovingly given me.

By end of July, I went for my fourth dilation procedure. This go-round proved more difficult than the previous ones without reason. After waking in the recovery room, I began to vomit blood and contorted with pain. The nurses were quick to react with pain and nausea medications. The doctor came in to check on me and soon the symptoms calmed. Frightened by this reaction, we had assurance that, while certainly requiring attention, the side effect was not uncommon.

The specialist checked me out and pronounced me ready for release. However, a statement he made as he walked away left us looking at each other dumbfounded. He mentioned that after the procedure I'd had two weeks before, he'd conferred with my surgeon to alert him to the fact the feeding tube appeared to be out of place. The specialist had felt the situation required immediate attention.

It became clearly apparent the surgeon had known problems existed with the feeding tube. Despite this knowledge, he'd left me to endure excruciating pain for two weeks without taking any action to correct the problem. It wasn't until I was in dire straights, virtually begging him to see me that this doctor took any action to relieve my agony. I could easily have died of the blockage that resulted from the simple slip of the feeding tube bulb while my pleas for help were ignored.

This information was the final straw. Our concerns involving the surgeon were abundant, seemingly growing by the day. Finding a new doctor was now imperative. The nurse's comments concerning the surgeon weighed heavily on our minds. We knew finding a bariatric surgeon who would consent to see another doctor's patient was going to be nearly impossible. We began calling the doctors listed as preferred providers by our insurance company. One by one they all refused to see me.

Still unable to tolerate solid foods, I could sustain only a bland clear liquid diet. As a result I remained dehydrated, malnourished, and in a constant state of exhaustion. Supplemental feedings twice daily, and weekly IV infusions kept me alive yet I continued to lose weight. Given the current situation, it would only be a matter of time before I simply starved to death. We were frustrated and very afraid. The surgeon's "magical thirteen-weeks" had come and gone, still nothing had changed. My life was in certain danger.

Family and friends hovered around me, terrified that I might not live to see another sunrise. In my own morbidly-depressed mind, I prepared myself for the inevitable end. I had made my peace with God and only worried for those left behind. It was a sobering notion, when you foretell death, yet knowing that in death is relief.

My husband continued his unwavering support and care for me, all the while enduring a private hell orchestrated by my surgeon. He never once let me see him falter. Later, friends would tell me how difficult the constant strain had been for him. A friend said that one afternoon he'd met my husband in the parking lot of a local department store and when asked how I was, he simply broke down in tears. It was terrifying to imagine my big, strong man crumbling; guilt consumed me knowing I was the cause of his pain.

I had a last ditch appointment with my surgeon on Friday, August 2, 2002. We explained my condition hadn't changed as well as the very dire concerns we had at my continual decline. My hair fell out in great tufts on my pillow, my teeth were loose (I had already lost two, that had simply crumbled in my mouth); I remained in a constant state of dehydration and malnourishment. Blood work revealed I was anemic and had considerable chemical imbalances, lacking in the acceptable levels of vitamins and nutrients. Nausea, vomiting, and pain continued to be a part of my daily life.

The surgeon mentioned he now suspected there might be a problem near the Y-junction of the intestine. No basis or explanation of this diagnosis followed. His intent involved changing the schedule to reserve a surgical suite for the following Thursday morning. Special permission and arrangements had to be made for several hospital departments to accommodate this procedure.

Before leaving the doctor's office that day, we requested a copy of my medical records, telling the receptionist we would wait for them. The receptionist knew the procedure and said the certified copy of my medical chart would follow in the mail within the next three to five business days. We rejected that offer. Again, we insisted on waiting for the copy of my chart. Suspiciously, we didn't want anyone to have an opportunity to modify the information in my records. After waiting for well over an hour, the receptionist informed us it was office policy that all requests for records must include a signed request form. Furthermore, the office required five to ten working days to produce the records. Then rather rudely, the receptionist stated that unless we had further business in the office, we should leave.

My husband was livid. His blood pressure would have registered—STROKE! We left the office and immediately called a cousin of mine who lived in the city to see if she knew an attorney who could help us obtain my records. She suggested someone who would be perfect for our needs. The attorney happened to be a friend of hers and she said, "He owed her a favor." The attorney dictated a quick letter demanding the release of my records to my husband immediately or the surgeon should prepare to answer a suit filed before the close of business that day. He faxed the letter to their office and suggested we return there.

I was physically exhausted. I remained at my cousin's home to lie down while my husband returned to the doctor's office to collect my records. The attorney had carefully worded the letter allowing my husband to act on my behalf. My husband carries a copy of my living will, so that he can make decisions concerning my care should I be incapacitated. After making my husband wait for over an hour, the receptionist finally complied with our request.

Strangely, several pages of another patient's chart were included in my records. Out of curiosity my husband read the pages. This patient had also experienced major complications from the surgery. He concluded from this brief review that her problems, like my own, were related to shortcomings on the part of the surgeon.

That very afternoon as we made our way home, we stopped in at a friend's restaurant. She had undergone gastric by-pass surgery several years past and mentored me during the research phase of my process. As I walked into the restaurant on trembling legs, she approached me immediately. She didn't even try to hide her alarm at my appearance. I looked like the walking dead, a zombie. It was obvious I was fading fast. We failed to realize how drastically things were about to change.

Chapter Ten

~ A FRIEND IN DEED ~

We hadn't planned to stop by my friend's restaurant that day; fate obviously led us there. On the way home, I had a sudden craving for her wonderful homemade mashed potatoes. I could usually eat them on good days when my system would allow me to eat at all. I had met this lady while doing research for surgery. I had no inkling that her presence in my life would have such a drastic impact.

She had undergone gastric by-pass surgery at a Florida university hospital several years before. Her weight had topped out in excess of four hundred pounds. The bulk was debilitating with many co-morbidities and physical limitations. Her story is amazing, the surgery was difficult for her but she had recovered splendidly. She is today less than half the woman she once was. She remains a wonderful source of information, support and friendship. Little did I know she would be the catalyst that saved my life.

When we walked through her door that day, she immediately approached to embrace me as she always did. This usually jovial soul hesitated at arm's length from me, almost afraid to touch me. My body was small and frail, words I had never expected to be associated with me. The horror and concern at my present condition was evident on her face. She bombarded us with questions concerning my health and the treatment I was receiving.

She insisted we allow her to contact the university surgeon who had performed her surgery and ask if he would see me. We knew this plan was a long shot at best. The surgeon wasn't accepting any new patients. We knew this because I had previously tried to get an appointment and was turned away. She bargained to get me an appointment using her personal relationship and long history with the university doctor. We were grateful she was willing to make the effort on my behalf, no matter how futile her attempt might be.

We experienced a great deal of mixed emotions. I knew this university doctor by reputation only. My friend placed the call immediately, amazingly, she knew the number by memory. We were stunned that within moments, the surgeon—not his nurse or receptionist or assistant or associate, but the surgeon was on the phone. This concept was foreign to us. We could barely get my own surgeon to return our calls. This man was an extremely busy doctor whose days involved seeing patients, performing surgery, instructing interns, teaching classes, and attending patients in the hospital, as well as seeing patients at the Veteran's Hospital. Yet, here he was on the phone discussing my case, not with another doctor but my friend, his patient.

She began the conversation with a very dramatic statement, none-the-less true. "Doc, my friend is dying before my eyes. Would you please see her?" After some back and forth discussion concerning my condition, and without ever speaking to me personally, he agreed to see me the very next day. Astonishment was an understatement, we were literally in shock. Not only did he agree to see me, but also this highly regarded surgeon would see me right away. We had no idea what to expect but for the first time in a very long time, we felt hope. This wonderful friend had taken a moment on my behalf and in doing so probably saved my life. We will be eternally grateful. We dared to hope that finally someone would help me live!

Very early the next morning, we set out on the trip to the university medical center, which was approximately two hours from our home. We were both relieved and nervous. Our emotions were running the gamut. We arrived armed with all of the medical intelligence we had gathered concerning my prior tests and medical file. Over the course of the drive, we discussed every aspect of my case and mentally prepared questions for this doctor. I was unable to walk under my own steam, nausea and pain continued to grip my body and my appearance was like a zombie on Halloween. My greatest fear was a confirmation of my surgeon's diagnosis, mental illness. In my heart, I felt as if no one, aside from my family and friends, believed the complications continually plaguing me were the result of the gastric by-pass surgery. It was obvious, at least to us that something was terribly wrong.

Thanks to a detailed map from the computer, we arrived at the huge university medical facility. The vast complex is comprised of the medical school, doctor's offices and the enormous hospital. We walked into the surgeon's waiting room, shocked that it was occupied by more than a hundred people. It appeared we were in for a very long wait. I checked in and obtained the usual clipboard with a ream of paperwork. Any reserve energy I had seemed to drain away right there. I felt overwhelmed by just the thought of muddling through these forms. The paperwork was extensive but by the time I had completed the first questionnaire, the nurse was calling my name. Our wait had been a total of twenty minutes from the time we had stepped off the elevator.

The mandatory vital signs routine were conducted, while another nurse hurriedly searched for a basin as nausea overwhelmed me. I doubled over in pain, straining while dry heaves contorted my body. The staff was quick to come to my aid; a cool cloth, water, a pillow and blanket as I was gently laid on the examining table. The staff was extremely attentive and caring. They went beyond all expectation, doing everything possible to comfort and care for me.

An intern, over the next thirty minutes, talked directly to my husband as he detailed the complications I had endured during the past five months. It was obvious I was in no shape to play twenty questions. The doctor entered the room, putting us immediately at ease. He'd read my medical chart and made it his first priority to let me know none of this was my fault. The pain and other complications were very real; not something merely conjured up in my brain. I cannot begin to explain how much this validation meant to me. He'd won my trust from the beginning. Even so, the psychological abuse inflicted by the original surgeon continues to leave a life-long mental scar.

The doctor first noted I was extremely malnourished and dehydrated. He wrote orders for my hospital admission immediately. At this point my weight was recorded at eighty-nine pounds. He explained that before he would even attempt any treatment, every effort had to be concentrated on stabilizing my condition. He felt I had some very real and serious medical conditions requiring immediate attention. He wanted to administer some tests to find out just where we stood. However, none of this would be possible now, I was simply too weak. The doctor explained that if left in this condition I had no possibility of survival. With hospital orders in hand, we declined an ambulance, knowing the hospital was less than half a mile away from the doctor's office. The doctor told us he would see us once I settled into a room.

The hospital is like a city unto itself. Imagine eight restaurants, a coffee shop, several gift shops, chapel, two banks, a barber and hairdresser as well as a state of the art medical facility. The sight was astounding. When we arrived for admission, I was quickly bundled into a wheelchair, whisked off to a room that was ready and waiting for me. We were shocked. The nurses immediately began scurrying around to hook up intravenous lines pumping fluids, vitamins, and nutrients to replenish my dehydrated body. Liquids were pumped into my feeding tube and blessed pain medication automatically fed intravenously on a set timetable. True to his word, the doctor checked in on me before sundown that evening.

After three days of intensive care and replenishment, the tests began from daylight until dawn. Over the following days, I had dozens of investigational medical tests. My husband was beside me all the way through. Some of the procedures were scary, some uncomfortable, and others seemed down right funny. One test involved my drinking three tiny test tubes of water, no more than a drop in each. There was no taste or texture, but we understood that liquid contained special isotopes, which would light up on an X-ray. This test would determine how my esophagus and digestion were working. The staff took special care so that I remained as physically comfortable as possible throughout. Many times, I simply slept through the entire process. Various interns checked on my progress three times a day and the doctor visited early each morning and late each evening. He explained every step in the process, why the tests were administered and the information he expected to glean from each one.

The results began flowing in and my wonderful new doctor, with his ever-present throng of interns on his heels, brought news of my first results. A few interns were fine but dealing with dozens of these eager medical students several times a day was beginning to wear on my nerves. I knew that I had the ability to request the interns not attend me but I never felt so annoyed with them that I would officially complain.

The ionic X-ray revealed I was having severe esophageal spasms, referred to as a "nut cracker" esophagus. The condition made it difficult, if not impossible, to swallow food properly. He ordered medication to soothe some of these spasms and I was allowed to consume clear liquids. However, what really troubled the doctor were the endoscopic results. The verdict "no evidence of a gastric pouch is apparent and the gastro-intestinal anatomy has been altered in an unconventional and questionable manner." The conclusion was that I had definitely not had a common *roux-en-y* surgery. The doctor spoke to us of either a reversal or revision surgery at some point in the future. However, he felt that in my current state of debilitation, I was in no condition to withstand any surgery unless measures became necessary to save my life. The extensive surgery he suggested would have to be postponed for at least a year.

The doctor scheduled a second endoscopic exam that he'd personally attend. Unfortunately, my over-used veins began to collapse. It seemed that nearly every nurse in the hospital had tried to thread an intravenous line. My arms looked like I'd been beaten black and blue. The nursing staff began to search for unconventional sites including between my fingers, my thumbs, my feet and toes then my neck.

As the midnight hour approached, a giant of a man walked through my hospital room door. He had to be six foot four or more, tipping the scales at an easy three hundred pounds. His appearance suggested intimidation, but nothing could be further from the truth. He was a very gentle giant. He performed IV's on the tiniest of all hospital patients in the neo-natal intensive care unit. Imagine this huge individual handling those little bodies, fitting effortlessly in the palm of his hand. The tender touch of this expert nurse placed miniscule needles into their threadlike veins. This wonderful man had come in from home, from his bed after a full shift at work, especially for me. His mission was to try to coax a thin IV needle into my failing veins.

His countenance was jolly and joking, while he went about his task where so many had failed. He made me feel instantly at ease. I had already been stuck more than ten times, but he was prepared to try one last time. He gathered the needed supplies, calling for a certain gauge needle. The gentle phlebotomist massaged my arms and legs, stroked my neck then declared that the only viable vein I had was in my foot, between my toes. Within moments, the needle was in place and he was on his way home to bed. A central line was threaded into the deep vein of my arm, the next morning. The multi-purpose line made the painful process of hunt and stick unnecessary.

The schedule called for a second endoscopic exam the next day. When I was wheeled into the room it was as crowded as a medical convention. My doctor, the usual posse of interns, the head of radiology and endoscopy departments as well as various nurses and attendants were all standing around waiting for the show to begin. The head of the endoscope department was the host of this shindig and I was the guest of honor. I was terrified because here at the university hospital this procedure called for the patient to be AWAKE. The official term was twilight sleep. I would have preferred the term, "knocked out cold."

The process lasted just over an hour. Afterward, the doctors conferred then spoke with my husband concerning their findings. The conclusion was that no significant stomach pouch was discernable; several area biopsies sampled the area to determine if any stomach material was unidentifiable but nonetheless, present.

The testing confirmed previous suspicions that the surgery was no standard *roux-en-y*. This was the third time this determination was reached by medical professionals. Apparently no stomach pouch existed but the doctors wouldn't definitely confirm this, only to say no stomach material was detected. We were very upset by the news but relieved to have some evidence concerning where my actual problems lay. The attending radiologist actually gave my husband digital pictures taken during the latest procedure.

The tests kept coming, it seemed they even invented more just for me. A smaller feeding tube replaced the present one. Then changes to my present medication regimen were ordered to better manage the debilitating pain and nausea. Scar tissue once again partially blocked my esophagus so a dilation procedure to reopen the narrowed pathway was scheduled.

After nearly a month in the university hospital, I was overjoyed to go home. I was anxious to be back among my own things, though still very weak, I felt somewhat better. An appointment was set for a follow-up visit in two weeks. In the meantime, my hero, the university doctor had given us his card listing his office number, pager number, private home number, as well as his email address. He informed us that should we have any questions or concerns, email would probably be the quickest manner to reach him. He checked his email continually throughout the day. He assured us that if we felt like the need to speak with him to feel free to call him using any of the numbers listed. He wanted an email update on my condition daily or at the very least every other day. We were in shock and somewhat skeptical. Never had a doctor been that available to us.

We quickly realized exactly where I stood with the original surgeon. Even after going to great lengths to specifically schedule the operating room, we hadn't heard a word from him or his office. Not a message on the answering machine inquiring on why I hadn't appeared for the procedure, no concerned call for a critically ill patient, nothing, no contact. We hadn't called to cancel the procedure because so much had been going on at the university hospital. Other than a statement each month demanding payment on my overdue balance, we didn't hear anything from my initial surgeon.

Strangely, I did hear from one nurse, the one who had shared with us the complaints of the surgeon's staff. She called on a weekly basis inquiring about my condition. I never spoke to her but on occasion, my husband did. She told him her call was strictly personal. She wasn't calling on behalf of the surgeon or his office. The caller ID confirmed this fact. She remained very concerned for my medical situation and me personally. After approximately six weeks, the calls suddenly stopped. We heard gossip she'd lost her job in the surgeon's office when it was discovered she was gathering information against him for a medical malpractice suit. The unsubstantiated story was the last we heard concerning the matter. I sincerely wished I had been included in some court case against this surgeon. I would have loved to face the man in court to reveal just the sort of medicine he practiced.

The only comments I've made publicly concerning my initial surgeon or surgery, was a nonspecific synopsis of complications, an overview of the medical treatments I had undergone, and a mention of the attitude taken by my original surgeon on a very popular obesity website. The statement was no more negative than that, certainly not libelous to anyone. At that time, I had never advised anyone to avoid this doctor. However, when asked specifically, I did counsel other people (who specifically asked) considering the surgery that choosing a surgeon is the most important factor in having gastric bypass surgery. I certainly never mentioned to anyone, outside my most intimate circle, the doctor considered my medical condition to be nothing more than a mental issue. I was so embarrassed by this suggestion I would never have discussed that allegation with anyone.

Within a week of updating my personal posting page concerning my current condition on the obesity website, I began receiving ugly emails. People I'd never met or had an email discourse with were calling me terrible names and leveling vicious accusations at me personally. The personal information noted in those emails could have only come from one source, my original surgeon's office. Details of my health issues were noted, including allegations of psychotic delusions. Verbal assaults charging that I refused to eat, that I was anorexic, striving for nothing more than sympathy and attention. I felt as though I were being personally attacked. We heard rumors that we, my husband and I, in an effort to cover up my mental illness, were vilifying the surgeon. The emailed abuse wounded me deeply.

My wonderful, constant support system refused to allow this situation to get the better of me. Intellectually, I realized there was no way to dissuade people who clearly believed this destructive surgeon's manipulation. He exploited people who felt grateful to him, using them to spread his venom without bringing any notice to him self. I took the only action possible in my defense by completely removing my personal and contact information posted on the obesity surgery support website.

I felt as if a huge door had been slammed in my face. Rejection by the gastric by-pass support group for truthfully telling my story left me feeling very alone. Nevertheless, people I'd never met, on-line or in person, knew medical facts about me that I'd never disclosed to anyone other than family and close friends. I was embarrassed, hurt and felt horribly violated. The slander leveled against me was the last straw for us. We began searching for an attorney to look into my case. I steeled myself against the emotional pain, bolstered by those people who meant the most to me. I might be a patient but I would not be a victim.

In September 2002, I had my second check-up with the university doctor. I had regained a little energy and was feeling better than I had in a very long time. Nausea and vomiting were still a part of my daily life; therefore, the doctor would not consider removing the feeding tube. He believed that because so much of my intestine had been removed (the original surgical notes stated that six feet of intestine rather than the normal two were removed), nutrient absorption would forever be a problem for me. He reiterated we were facing either a revision or a reversal surgery, yet still he didn't feel I was physically strong enough to withstand further surgery. My university surgeon advised us that our ultimate goal was to keep my health as stable as possible so I would be able to undergo corrective surgery when the time was right.

The severe nausea and vomiting continued, so my university doctor scheduled another endoscope and dilation procedure as an outpatient one week later. I was terrified. This procedure was painful, frightening and the mere thought of going through it with only the aid of a "slight relaxant" stressed me to the core. No matter how I tried to prepare myself mentally for the procedure, the reality was that the procedure was painful and scary.

My weight held steady for approximately six weeks. Utilizing every feminine ruse in my repertoire, I begged, cajoled, and cried until I finally convinced my doctor to remove the offensive feeding tube. The tube, which hung down about four inches, pulled when I dressed or undressed. When the raw incision in my belly felt the tension of the pulled tube, the sudden pain would make me see stars.

Several weeks later in October 2002, I finally accomplished my mission and the feeding tube took its final exit (for a while anyway). My doctor cautioned that at any time I showed significant weight-loss (more than five pounds), the feeding tube would have to be reinserted. I was ecstatic and ignored that last rule. I was so excited I could take a regular shower for the first time in a very long time. Sink baths were sufficient but did little to really make one feel clean.

I continued to have some nausea and vomiting but even though it was unimaginable, I had learned to deal with the problems as part of my daily grind. I felt better now. My diet excluded many foods, which were primary sources of protein. I simply could not tolerate solid proteins like meat.

My sister progressed well. As a teacher, she had seven weeks of recovery after surgery and was ready to assume her duties when school started. She was losing weight with only the most common complaints. I am so proud for her. Even through her own recovery, she still worried about me. We talked on the telephone, endlessly comparing what we could and could not eat. My consumption was limited to soups and soft foods while my sister had already graduated to solid food without problem.

We commiserated about vomiting, gas, diarrhea, and constipation. "Normal" bowel movement was often the topic of the day. Weren't these common points of conversation for everyone? Gross bodily functions were standard exchange for us. Our dialog always began with the same question, "What did you eat today?" I tried to keep my complication complaints to a minimum. I knew my sister felt guilty she was doing well and I was still suffering. In my estimation, the surgical complication rate of one out of two, are not such good odds.

Chapter 11

~ LIFE GOES ON ~

The once joyful Yuletide season arrived and quietly slipped away. The holiday went practically unnoticed in our household. We managed to make our usual tedious route to visit our families, but it was far from the festive traditional celebration of our youth. The holiday circuit usually encompasses the better part of three days and speeds by in a blur, leaving us wishing for just a little more time to spend with our loved ones. However, this season the trip consumed all of my reserved energy. By the second day of our travel, I began to seriously question if this visit was wise at all. My fragile state was quickly dissolving.

On the other hand, seeing everyone I love made me feel as though I was normal for the first time in a very long time. That is at least whatever normal was for me. I was no more miserable than usual. It is an awful revelation when a good day is simply being able to withstand the pain, manage to dress myself, overcome the debilitating fatigue, and control the nausea. Then if I'm having an exceptionally good day, I'm able to stand the gut-wrenching gas spasms long enough to have a brief conversation.

I slept through the majority of our visits but it was simply an amazing feat that I had left our home for somewhere other than the hospital. The best gift of all that Christmas season was the fact I had survived to see another year. Unfortunately, the look on our families' faces, as they openly stared, was gruesome. The consensus was I could very well be celebrating my last Christmas among them. Most everyone took some individual time with me, in case my days were growing short.

My eyes disappeared into darkened bruise-rimed recesses in my skull. Flesh hung loosely on my frame; my bones were clearly defined just beneath translucent, blotched, dry and peeling skin. Crimson red welts marked my entire body. The blood blisters resulted from, simply put, starvation. In essence my body had begun to feed on its own tissue to leach the calories and nutrients unavailable to me through the most common source—food. Malabsorption was then, and continues to be, one of my chief medical complications since the surgery.

Just after Christmas, I summoned enough courage to try going back to work part-time. The Herculean effort was brave but not very smart. I so wanted to get my life back in order and with the help of the sweetest people in the world, my co-workers. I did experience a few good days. There were days when I was so sick, one of guys would insist on driving me home. My situation was often embarrassing when I would not even have enough strength to walk from my desk to the parking lot. My co-workers were always there for me. They would have done anything for me and I truly love them for their care and concern.

It slowly became glaringly obvious just how fragile my body had become. In mere minutes, my health could decline so seriously that an ambulance had to be summoned numerous times to speed me away to the nearby hospital. I was quickly becoming a liability in our office, because clearly, being there was putting my health at risk. It also exposed the men to a precarious situation where I might collapse in the office and they might not be able to revive me. Our supervisor thought it best I not come into the office again until my health improved, drastically improved.

Finally, out of fear and frustration, I requested disability retirement forms from our human resources department. I had decided to at least find out exactly what filing the paperwork entailed. I needed to know what my options were. Though my co-workers were supportive, upper management was beginning to take a dim view of my constant absences. Honestly, it was understandable from their point of view. For the longest time, the retirement package remained untouched. Every time I felt too tired, weak, nauseous or my body contorted in pain to the point I was unable to complete even the smallest task, I'd slide the paperwork out of the envelope and look at it again.

The thick sheaf of papers seemed to call my name, taunting me. Every time my eye caught a glimpse of the official-looking manila envelope, I felt terrible guilt. I had brought this situation upon myself, voluntarily. After all, that is why it's called "elective surgery". I struggled with the decision to apply for a disability retirement for an exceptionally long time. I weighed my options and then enacted my other intense compulsion (besides the eating compulsion that landed me in this situation to begin with); I made a list of the pros and cons. The conclusion was soon to be out of my hands.

Heading the list in favor of disability was the fact that this option was a much better alternative to termination, which was definitely a possibility if my situation wasn't soon resolved. A healthy resolution didn't look likely in the near future. One by one I began to analyze the other options. I was really stalling for time instead of facing the obvious. I finally came to the conclusion that in my heart I felt applying for disability was admitting defeat. In that case I would be letting this terrible condition get the better of me. A defeatist attitude revealed weakness and that is simply not in my nature. By example, my parents had instilled in me a strong character and even stronger work ethic but my energy was fading fast.

The short span of semi-manageable health did not last through the New Year. The morning of December 28, I reported for work not feeling too bad. I am a morning person, which often irritates those who are not. I had no appetite—nothing unusual there, so I simply drank my morning coffee. About halfway through the cup I began to feel nauseous, this was obviously not going to be one of my good days. Suddenly a very intense knife-like pain stabbed my right side. I tried to relieve the sharp cutting blows by walking. The pain refused to subside. I was determined to beat this. I tried to ignore the pain as much as possible, yet nothing seemed to bring any relief. The piercing agony demanded my full attention. As I walked toward my boss, his first words were, "Do you need an ambulance or a driver?" My face bore a mask of misery.

The question was not if I needed medical attention but how I wanted to achieve that end. Our local hospital was less than two miles away, therefore I felt as if I could make it on my own. Pardon the pun, but we had been down this road before. If the worst happened, I did have my cell phone. Unbeknown to me, my boss had one of my co-workers follow me. As soon as I sat down in the car, I called my husband to let him know I was headed to the emergency room and to please meet me there. Tears coursed down my cheeks, as I questioned my ability to drive. But I gritted my teeth, praying that I'd arrive at my destination before I passed out.

I didn't bother with a parking spot, leaving my car with the keys still in the ignition by the curb closest to the door. I staggered into the deserted emergency waiting room but true-to–form, it was mandated to follow procedure. Before the admitting nurse would even speak to me, I was obliged to sign in and wait for my name to be called. I could barely stand then, as a wave of torment filled my senses, I collapsed like a rag doll to the floor. I soon found that this action is the key to getting noticed in the emergency room.

Still, the nurse insisted on putting me through the arduous check-in process completing the insurance papers and such. My patience was wearing thin. I felt as if I were about to come mentally unhinged. Who cares when my birthday is, what my social security number is, where I live or my phone number? All of that information was in their computers, it's not like I hadn't made this trip before, matter-of–fact, it wasn't even the first time in the last month. I wanted drugs, strong ones, and I wanted them NOW!

When they asked for a urine specimen, much to my surprise and that of the attending nurse, a stone thumped into the cup. My husband had hastily arrived very soon after me, even though he had more than twice the distance to travel. I really don't know how fast and reckless he drove to get there and I don't think I want to know. We were informed that I was to be immediately admitted, and then once the arrangements were made, I would be transferred to a much larger hospital facility to the south. I required the attention of a specialized urologist, advanced diagnostic and treatment equipment not available in our small town hospital. Pain medication was administered, which took effect rather quickly, relieving my tortured body with blissful unconsciousness.

My mind ebbed and receded, in and out like the tide to the shore. Through a drugged haze, I had no concept of passing time, as I was loaded into the ambulance, sometime later. I could hear someone talking to me but the voice was distant and I couldn't tell who it was or interpret what was said. Somewhere in my mind, there was a blaring siren and I felt the gurney respond to bumps in the road. Beyond those vague thoughts, nothing penetrated the drug-induced cloud.

Looking back, we think of the days spent in that large medical facility as a week in hell. The chief purpose for transferring me there was the availability of a lithotripsy machine to crush my huge collection of kidney stones. I had passed two additional sizable stones. Amazingly, I had yet to see a doctor, any doctor, since leaving our hometown hospital. It was in these dire straits that I spent the New Year's holiday. Happy 2003!

My sorely-abused veins began to burst after the first two days in the hospital. Because the nurses had no formal orders from a doctor to proceed with any other course of action other than intravenously, this put an end to all treatment. I was completely cut off: no fluids for rehydration, no vitamins to battle the malabsorption, no pain medication to ease my suffering, and no nutritional supplements to provide some source of energy. Soon I was spiking a fever, which even someone with no medical training knows indicates an infection. Still no medical treatment was forth coming, not even a Tylenol to bring my temperature down.

I was somewhat delirious, my husband was livid. The fever and pain spiraled out of control. The nurses could offer no comfort other than continuing their attempts to contact the doctor. We began to question why I was here at all. Without treatment, I could lie in bed at home and not be charged more than one thousand dollars a day hospital expenses. My husband was soon a force to be reckoned with. He first spoke to the head nurse, then proceeded to contact the patient relations office and finally requested an appointment with the hospital administrator; still nothing happened. Patient relations informed us that if I were taken out of the hospital without a formal doctor's dismissal, my insurance company would not pay for the hospital stay at all. We felt as if I were being held captive. After a week of this abuse, my husband had come to his wit's end. He demanded a resolution to this predicament immediately. Again the nurses promised us that the doctor would arrive soon. He didn't.

A cheerful stranger walked into my room and took a seat beside my bed. We'd never met the big burly man dressed in a white lab coat but erroneously assumed he was a kidney specialist. We explained my recent problems with kidney stones in detail and were told I was here to have the stones crushed. We were puzzled when he asked, "Then why am I here?" We soon found out the urologist who was supposedly handling my case determined, without ever meeting or examining me, that I required a gastric specialist rather than an urologist, based on my past medical history. No tests were conducted in order for the urologist to make this determination, nor was I ever even the same room with him. The gastric doctor was horrified at my present situation. He stepped into the hall and screamed, I mean he truly yelled down the hall to the nurses' station, ordering them to call the urologist immediately! In an attempt to calm the doctor, the nurses explained they'd paged the doctor, called his office and cell phone numbers numerous times with no results. The excuses only served to further infuriate the gastric doctor. He responded, quite angrily, for the nurses to call the doctor at home. Loudly and with great gusto, he shouted, "Doctors all live in houses". He then returned to my bedside and asked if in the meantime I needed anything. I weakly pleaded for pain medication. He saw to it that the medicine was administered right away. I never saw this doctor again and can't to this day recall his name. We felt as if we had met our savior yet hours passed with no further word from the nurses or the urologist. My very brief respite had given us hope then just as quickly, salvation was gone again.

In frustration my husband called both our family doctor and my university physician to see what could be done to get me released from this hospital. My doctors acted very quickly. Within thirty minutes the nurses informed me I was to be released with instructions to see my general physician the next day. We left the facility without ever having seen the urologist.

However, for the next five years, the urologist continued to send us a sizable bill each and every month. We reported his fraudulent claim to our insurance company, including the circumstances involved during this traumatic hospital stay. To date, they have neither acknowledged, nor taken any action in this case of obvious medical neglect and fraudulent insurance claims.

During the early days of February 2003, tragedy struck our family. Suddenly, without warning, my husband's dear mom unexpectedly collapsed at home. And sadly, my beloved mother-in-law passed away. She had been a source of constant support for all of her children and when I married her only son, she welcomed me into the fold. Mom had continually called to keep tabs on my health, letting me know of her concern and she thought of me often. Her loss was deeply felt by the entire family and I still miss her very much. The days, weeks and months following her untimely death steeped the entire family in grief.

The waning days of February found me again in the office of my general physician. He referred me to a local urologist who was willing to see me right away to handle the recent kidney stone problem. I was to report to the radiology department of our local hospital for X-rays to diagnose exactly what we were dealing with. During the process, I could tell by the way the radiologist acted that something was amiss. She was not allowed to discuss what she had seen with me but had to hand over the X-rays so my doctor could read them. He would explain the results and the best way to proceed given the diagnosis. On our way back to his office, I peaked at the X-rays, but alas, the cloudy black and white film negatives meant nothing to me.

The urologist explained to us I was producing what was

commonly called, "cluster kidney stones." These stones were the result of my inability to take in enough fluids to flush the sand-like crystals from my kidneys. The malabsorption issues exasperated the situation. Further testing required I take a jug home and measure the amount of urine I passed during a twenty-four hour period. He prescribed several medications to help soothe my aching kidney spasms. The jug test revealed that because of my constant state of dehydration, my kidney output equaled approximately one and a half cups of urine per day. Normal output should have totaled more than a half-gallon.

Within a very few days, the kidney pain became intolerable and I was admitted to the hospital on March 13, 2003. Coincidentally, this date was the first anniversary of my gastric by-pass surgery. The urologist entered my hospital room with a concerned look on his face. He sat down on the edge of my bed and patted my knee to reassure me. We held our breath because obviously the results weren't good.

The testing showed more than thirty kidney stones, some so large I could never pass them without assistance. We were given several options. First, the stones could be left and medication given to combat the pain, unfortunately, in doing this, we risked a debilitating urinary tract infection. Second, the urologist could shoot the largest of the stones with a laser to break them up. The complication was that the kidneys would be left severely bruised and bleed. I would still have to pass the sandy remains of the stones if the laser was employed but there was one more option which involved the urologist manually retrieving the largest of the stones with a specially designed basket. The last option carried with it the standard risks of surgery.

Fear of infection and taking into consideration my already depleted body, the urologist required that I receive a course of intravenous antibiotics before any treatment could commence. Together with the doctor we decided, based on my weakened condition, he should try to break up the stones with the laser. He told us that before I could be released from the hospital, it was essential to pump me with fluids to relieve the dangerous state of dehydration. Remaining in my present condition could result in renal failure. Should my kidneys fail, I would have to begin dialysis. Ten pain-filled days later, I was finally allowed to return home to my family.

The procedure to crush the stones was done in outpatient surgery. Under twilight sleep, the procedure lasted about forty-five oblivious minutes. After a nice dose of pain medication that forestalled the eventual ache following the procedure, I slept the entire ride home.

Reality slapped me full force when I finally awoke. I felt as if a heavy weight boxer went twelve rounds on my back flanks. Bruised and sore, I didn't want to move or breathe. Though given ample warning concerning the after-math of surgery, and then mentally preparing myself for the reaction, when you urinate blood, regardless of preparation, it's frightening. Wiping my tender private parts was like using sandpaper. Tears welled in my eyes every time I felt the urge to go to the bathroom. The latest torture took eight full days to run its course.

I tried again to return to work, however, my health continued to interfere. More than one supervisor spoke to me about applying for disability retirement. I made the call and had the paperwork sent to me for a second time. The men I worked with were the most supportive and amazing guys. In an attempt to fatten me up some, they would often come to work with my breakfast favorites. One made a truly delectable potato soup and a very special individual asked me everyday, "Want some candy, little girl?" These men continue to remain very special to me. Though there was not a great deal I would miss concerning my career, my co-workers were always fantastic to me.

As I made my way home from work one afternoon, I began to feel very nauseous and my hands trembled uncontrollably. The feeling was unnerving. My mind became muddled. I couldn't seem to concentrate as I struggled to drive. I slowed the vehicle to a mere crawl, trying desperately to cover the short distance to our home. I feared I might pass out behind the wheel and was terrified. I could barely walk in the house on shaky legs and quickly realized no one was home to assist me.

Something had to be done and I had to handle it alone. I still had no idea what was happening to me. It took me nearly ten minutes to place a call to our family doctor, the thought to call 911 never occurred to me. Darkness began to encroach and narrow my field of vision. His nurse came on the line and I explained my situation as best I could. By this time I was weeping, confused, and unable to think clearly. She immediately identified my symptoms as low blood sugar. This wonderful nurse instructed me to slowly sip orange juice with two tablespoons of sugar mixed in. She spoke to me slowly with a very calming tone. The nurse would call every five minutes until I began to feel better. If my condition had not improved within thirty minutes, she would call an ambulance. We hung up the phone for the first time then she immediately called my husband on his cell phone, relating the situation and instructing him to get home as soon as possible. Within moments my symptoms began to abate. True to her word, she called me every five minutes.

Still, the summer had additional medical emergencies in store for us. In June 2003 (again during the week of my birthday), I was rushed from work by one of my co-workers to the local emergency room. I spent eight hours lying in agony receiving pain medication and passing kidney stones. By days' end, I had passed five ugly, burred stones but still the hospital felt there was no reason to keep me. We should be accustomed to this treatment by now, right!

The next morning I passed six more stones mixed with a considerable amount of blood. My husband was beyond frustrated. By the last days of June, I was admitted to the northern hospital for kidney stones again. I was losing considerable blood, having the semi-rare AB positive blood type, the transfusion became somewhat of an ordeal. Most people faced with kidney stones would be debilitated and beyond agony, however, the situation was becoming terribly common for me.

My urologist suggested I begin receiving IV fluid replacement once a week to help flush out my kidneys. The stones were beginning to weaken my kidneys. They were threatening to shut down. My tenuous hold on health couldn't afford failing kidneys on top of everything else. Repeated infections from the constant irritation were doing considerable irreversible damage. The potent antibiotics caused yeast infections in my mouth and intimate area. The infection burned and itched terribly and my mouth was completely raw, making it difficult to eat. Though I had put on a little weight in the preceding months, my weight now began to drop dangerously fast.

The urologist suggested that I have a central line implanted so the visiting nurses wouldn't have to stick me over and over again each week. My veins were so over used, they were hardly viable anymore. We were agreeable to this, being a human pincushion was no fun at all.

The weekly saline drip was fortified with vitamins and nutrients to keep me hydrated in an attempt to flush the stones through the urinary system and to help battle my continuing malabsorption issues. During this time, I continued to pass three to five stones per week. Sometimes the pain was manageable and others, it took all the efforts at our disposal to get the intensive pain under some semblance of control. The urologist ordered kidney X-rays every six weeks to keep track of the stones. I still keep the stones I pass in a jar, everyone asks when I plan to come up with a line of jewelry featuring them.

When I finally had enough strength to manage washing my hair, handfuls of the long strands began to clog the drain. Once, in my prime, I had a thick mass of dark brunette hair which now lay thin and limp, my scalp clearly exposed through the white translucent cover. Although my fingernails continued to grow, they do so in the oddest shapes curling toward my finger tips. These problems, thinning hair and curling nails, are just another sign of protein malabsorption and malnutrition. Additionally, perhaps the most embarrassing instance came when my two front teeth broke when I gently nibbled on a pretzel. The gaps made my smile that of a first grade student or perhaps a gapped-toothed jack-o-lantern.

All these complications can be linked to the gastric bypass surgery and to a word we continued to hear over and over again, malabsorption. Lack of protein and calcium were the major complications causing my hair, nails and teeth problems. Constant dehydration left my skin flaky and peeling, my kidneys were unable to flush waste and bowel impactions distended and herniated my colon. Dark bruised circles surrounded my sunken eyes, classic in gastric by-pass patients, lent me a look of emaciation and ailing. If the truth be known, I was simply starving to death as a direct result of the surgery.

Because I had experienced a great deal of chronic pain in my lower back, my family doctor suggested I have a bone scan to see where we were at this point. He called this first scan a baseline. It would be used in the future to note the progress of my deteriorating bones. The test, no more uncomfortable than a standard X-ray, revealed significant bone deterioration in several discs in my back—early onset osteoporosis as well as a pinched nerve on my right lumbar flank and hips. Of course, more medication followed but beyond that nothing could be done. Usually the doctor would prescribe additional calcium supplements to help fight the deficiency, however, he was reluctant to do so due to the fact I was producing an over abundance of kidney stones. A chewable calcium supplement was our only alternative at this point, however, because of the malabsorption it still left me lacking considerably.

People who have had kidney stones say this is the closest pain to childbirth that anyone will ever experience. Having gone through two pregnancies with natural childbirth, that is to say, using only minimal medication, I can tell you passing a kidney stone is much, much worse than childbirth. Doctors are taught, and truly believe, that it is medically impossible to feel pain without the stones moving through the urinary system. Most patients will tell you this just isn't the case. The pain may not be as intense but the lower back pain, stinging urination, and the body just hurts when stones are present. Kidney stone patients often refer to the pain as if they were passing razor blades when urinating. This may sound dramatic, however, believe me, it's a pretty accurate description. I firmly believe that all urologists should have to pass at least one stone to qualify to treat patients with stones. It isn't until they endure the stones that the doctor can truly understand the excruciating pain their patients go through. Of course, my urologist doesn't agree.

My urologist determined that it was necessary to insert a stint into my ureter, the tube extending from the kidney to the bladder. The stint would keep that passageway open wide enough to allow kidney stones to pass with lessened pain. I was also prescribed a medication that would lessen the spasms in my urinary tract. The procedure of placing the stint was not all that complicated. It was done again under twilight sleep. The placement was considered outpatient surgery and I was home that afternoon.

I really couldn't feel the stint but did notice a small leaking of urine. At first the leakage was only a few drops, therefore a simple pad took care of this minor irritation, no big deal. Well, a minor irritation until … the stint slipped! Where did it slip to, you might ask? Though the situation seems quite humorous now, it was not at all amusing at the time. The stint had slipped into my bladder, keeping it constantly open. And what does that mean? It was like turning on a faucet, I was constantly flowing urine and not in a small amount. A pad was useless; a bucket would have been more helpful. I couldn't sit on my furniture without a puddle forming beneath me. I had to put plastic down to protect my couch and mattress. I was holding a towel between my legs to sop up the constant flow. It was awful.

I placed a frantic call to the urologist's service because, of course, this happened as usual after office hours. The service paged him and assured us he'd return the call as soon as possible. The wait was intolerable. I was terrified something was seriously wrong and minutes dragged into hours. When the phone finally rang, it was my best friend doing her usual daily buddy check. I explained that we'd talk later. I was frantic to speak to the doctor. Having a very sensitive stomach and a low tolerance for the disgusting side of my problems, I avoided the more graphic details to my friend. She is very adept at determining how bad things are with minimal details at the very tone of my voice.

The phone shrilled again. Hurriedly, I raced to the receiver. This time the caller was my sister and I explained to her in great detail—she can take it—what was going on with me. She had great sympathy and remarkably, we cut the call short. This was the first call we've ever had that lasted less than an hour, so that I could impatiently wait for the urologist to return my desperate summons.

Within twenty minutes, the ringing of the phone broke the baited silence. It was finally the urologist. I explained my most recent complication. The doctor informed me this was quite common and really no big deal. The stint had slipped into my bladder, which was being kept open and until the stint was removed, the bladder would constantly drain. My options involved pulling the stint out myself, rushing to the emergency room to remove the stint or wait until Monday morning when the doctor could remove the offensive medical implement. He further explained removing the stint myself, which was not difficult, would probably make the most sense. "You want me to do what?" was my basic reaction. Though I felt very nervous at the idea of this, he explained to me how to go about removing it. The directions sounded easy enough, but I was still filled with trepidation.

I washed my hands with anti-bacterial soap and put on latex gloves. I sat on the toilet and bore down slightly then I felt for a string much like that of a tampon. Sorry men, this is only a small facet of a woman's life here. One firm tug, according to the doctor, should release the stint. I tentatively pulled on the string and felt immediate pain, letting go very quickly. The doctor had said nothing about grit your teeth and cry. I took a deep breath and tried again. This time I took a firmer stance and pulled on the string with a jerk. With a shock of pain, the stint came out. It really wasn't much more difficult than pulling out a tampon or for those guys out there who haven't experienced that special unique action, maybe removing a cork from a bottle except for the popping sound. Although there was some pain involved, it diminished fairly quickly.

I was astonished to see what had given me so much trouble. It was an elongated repeatedly curved S-shaped wire covered with soft plastic tapering from a large curve to a smaller one. The urine faucet was turned off for the most part but my bottom was burning considerably. The urologist said this would pass. I was amazed and showed the stint to everyone in the house. No one seemed as intrigued with it as I was. And no one was more overjoyed that it had been removed.

In October 2003, I visited the hospital for follow-up X-rays of my kidneys to check on the progress of my stones. I still passed one to five painful stones per week, some as tiny as a grain of rice and others the size of an English pea. The test revealed my body was replenishing the supply of kidney stones nearly as fast as I was passing them. I basically had beanbags where my kidneys once were. That is a weak attempt to laugh through the pain. Another lithotripsy was scheduled for the next week. The urologist explained this procedure would be the last he could perform for at least six months. The delay allowed for the kidneys to heal from the intense trauma of the procedure. The treatment could irreparably damage my kidneys if done too often or too many times.

Another year faded away. I was simply thankful to be alive. However, I was still very weak, depleted and dehydrated. Still, I was losing a massive amount of weight and generally feeling awful. I could rarely eat anything except soft foods such as grits and mashed potatoes but with such a limited diet, soon you don't want to see another bowl of soup or scrambled egg again in your entire life. Eating became a chore, a burden that was sometimes just too cumbersome to bear. Depression was a constant state of being for me. I lived with fear for my life every day.

Over and above what I felt, my children were terrified that each time they spoke to me might be their last. This was a stab to my heart like no other. Both of my sons lived several hours away from me and each was going through a silent hell, worried for their mother. My dad and sister, some of my husband's family, and our dear close friends called to get the daily report. The news never seemed to be very good. I hated always complaining so I began to avoid the phone, leaving the medical reports to my husband. He was outwardly a rock for me but emotionally, he was torn apart and physically, he was exhausted. He often lay awake at night and watched me breathe, like one might do with an infant. Then during the day, my dear husband jumped at every sound I made. When I slept in our bed, he positioned his office chair where he could watch me from his desk. No one should have to live the way we were forced to exist. We had stopped living and began a constant struggle to merely survive.

Chapter Twelve

~ *SURVIVAL* ~

As 2003 ended, my immediate supervisor informed me time had run out and I had to make an immediate decision about my future. Notified to either return to work full time, resign, retire or risk termination added immense pressure. The decision, as if I had any options, was a limited time offer. Upper management was pressuring my supervisor because it appeared I was now unfit to perform the duties of my job description. Looking back over the past year, I had worked less than one hundred twenty hours. I could request an official leave of absence (which at this point probably would not be approved on the grounds I might never be able to return to work full time) or apply for a medical retirement. Based on these options, a medical retirement was my only hope. If denied my disability retirement, I would soon be terminated and have no recourse but to go on public assistance.

A medical retirement would give me some income, which was more than I had now. The most desirable aspect of retirement, the only favorable point unless you count the part about no termination, would be my ability to maintain the medical and life insurance coverage I now carried. The paperwork was extensive, requiring statements from me, my immediate supervisor, as well as every doctor who had attended me. It could take a considerable span of time to have the retirement approved, however, no action could be taken against me during the process. Given the alternative, I placed a call to our human resources department and for a third time I requested the medical retirement paperwork package. I felt sure the human resources department was tired of repeatedly sending me this information.

We were fortunate, in that my husband owns his own business, had he worked for someone else, he would be out of a job as well. His time involved caring for me so he worked only sporadically, however, the price was still a bitter pill to swallow. Ultimately, his business lost approximately thirty percent of its clientele. I was unable to care for myself, let alone drive while under the influence of the various prescription medications. Repeated doctor's visits, hospital stays, and emergency room runs filled our days and nights.

With the help of our families, we paid only the minimum monthly payments in order to keep our home, vehicles, as well as keep our utilities functioning and vehicle insurance. Of course, our family was accustomed to eating on a regular basis, so groceries were somewhat of a necessity and my medication was an unavoidable expense. All of our credit cards were over their limits because a great deal of the time we depended on them to live. The expense total escalated rather quickly, especially when I was in the hospital and my husband was eating fast food at every meal. Many times, when money was hard to come by, he ate his meals from a hospital vending machine using what little change he found in his pocket.

Many nights, when my beloved husband was unable to stay with me in the hospital and unable to pay for a hotel, he was forced to sleep in his truck in the hospital parking garage. Of course, "camping out" there was against hospital policy but security was kind to him and looked the other way. There were times when the security guards would bring him dinners from the hospital cafeteria because they knew he had no money to eat. Every evening the guards would inquire about my condition, we will be forever grateful for their kindness.

Creditors, bill collectors, and collection agencies began calling our home every morning around seven a.m. and continued to call until sometimes eleven p.m. After repeated admonishment, criticism, cajoling, and threats repeatedly every day, we simply stopped answering the phone. My husband began screening all of our calls through the caller ID and either let the answering machine answer the phone or claimed we were not at home. The callers threatened more collection agencies, ruined credit, garnishment, and court proceedings. They would take away our birthdays if possible! We realized these people were just doing their jobs, however, after you have explained the situation three hundred times, what else is there to say? We'd written letters to all our creditors explaining in detail the problems we were facing and had enclosed a letter from my university surgeon verifying our claim. The calls continued as if we were simply refusing to pay the bills we owed. Many of the collectors were very cruel and said ugly, hurtful things. One man suggested my husband have me committed to a nursing home facility run by the state.

We owned nothing of real value to sell or for our creditors to take, except perhaps our home and somehow, we had managed to stay only one payment behind on that. We had no income to garnish, so that left us somewhere between the proverbial rock and a hard place. The only way we managed to stay afloat at all was through our wonderful families and friends, we will never be able to repay what they so freely gave. Our hearts are full of love for their commitment to us.

I had very good medical insurance, however, deductibles, co-payments, and expenses over and above what the insurance covered had begun to mount drastically. The hospitals, doctors, labs, and medication bills were soaring out of control. The amount we owed after our insurance had paid was well above two hundred thousand dollars by the end of 2003. The figure continued to rise daily. Some of my medication cost astronomical prices … three of the pills I depended on daily cost several hundred dollars per dose. Then there were the extremely potent antibiotics that amounted to several thousand dollars per treatment.

I managed to spend Christmas of 2003 at home, but there would be no family trek for us this year. I was simply too weak to travel and due to the pain medication, I was not aware of my surroundings anyway. Within three days of Christmas, I was back in the hospital with kidney stones. I spent New Years' Eve in the hospital watching the ball drop in Times Square on television with my exhausted husband asleep in the chair beside my bed. I was extremely grateful to be alive as 2003 passed into history. By January 1, 2004, 12:01 a.m., I had already met my health insurance deductible of $500.00 for the year and the balances for medical care continued the skyward ascent.

I was set to see our family doctor in mid-January. Lab orders in hand I actually walked into the hospital before my appointment for blood work and X-rays. Again, the news was not good. However, now it appeared the terrible test results were "normal" for me. Anemia, dehydration, and malabsorption were all exacting a considerable toll on my body. The tests told a story of self-preservation, my body had begun to feed on itself almost constantly now.

The daily allowance of calcium required for a healthy body now came from my existing bones and teeth. The follow-up bone scan results showed a significant deterioration when compared to the baseline scan taken just a few months before. Several small hairline fractures appeared on my right ankle and hip. My body ached constantly; there were times when I would simply break down into heart-wrenching sobs out of pain, fear, and frustration. The majority of my bones were very brittle, even honeycombed in some areas. The doctor cautioned me to exercise extreme care to avoid breaks during regular daily activities. When I say regular activities, those involved stepping out of the tub, rolling over in bed, or simply bending to pet the dog.

My teeth were continually chipping away, jagged stubs leaving a gapping crevice where my smile once had been. Several molars were loose and falling out piece by piece. I was so self-conscious I felt I could not speak without covering my mouth to hide the shame.

As if that were not enough, several days later I awoke with red welts covering my legs and abdomen. Another frantic call to our family physician followed. He agreed to meet us at his office on a Sunday … these emergencies never seemed to crop up during regular business hours. The diagnosis was a condition called petechiae. The problem was uncommon. I had experienced very small patches of the raised red splashes across my skin, however, now I looked simply dreadful and refused to allow my husband to peer at my grotesque body.

The petechiae, in this instance, were concentrated on my legs and torso. The doctor explained this was a result of a protein deficiency. My body was taking the needed protein from connective tissues beneath the skin resulting in spotted hemorrhages. There was no treatment available for this condition but in some cases, it indicated a lack of blood platelets, a blood infection or sepsis. The lack of blood platelets called for a blood transfusion and sepsis required massive doses of extremely potent antibiotics. Eventually, all of these treatment options became repeatedly necessary. The doctor began with writing orders for a blood transfusion and two additional units of blood platelets in hopes of avoiding a major crisis.

Every Wednesday, just like clockwork, the home health care nurses arrived at our home to administer fluids and other intravenous medications. After nearly constant use, my veins were no longer viable. The central line had swelled and festered, obviously infected so the doctor had no choice but to remove it. As a result, the nurses would at times subject me to six or more puncture attempts before they successfully found a viable vein. Shortly thereafter, the veins either collapsed or blew and the nurse started from the beginning once again. They felt horrible at having to put me through the repeated attempts to secure an IV and I felt sorry for the nurses as I watched them agonize with each unsuccessful attempt.

After repeated unintentional abuse, I finally spoke to our family doctor on the recommendation of my visiting nurse concerning a permanent central line. I would not have to endure the involuntary inflicted pain and the home health care nurses would have an easier job in taking care of me.

Bruises vividly stood out in a rainbow of the color spectrum from black and blue to the fading yellow and green spread along the tender skin of my arms. Our family doctor agreed that a permanent catheter was definitely called for in my case. He referred me to a local surgeon to discuss and schedule the outpatient surgery. I was relieved and nervous as well. I'd never had this kind of catheter and didn't know what was involved. The surgeon determined the weekly fluid infusion would be a long-term process to assist in flushing my kidneys in an effort to keep them as healthy as possible. Therefore, a central line was medically necessary.

Later that same afternoon, the local surgeon's office called saying the doctor could see me the following day. I was shocked at the suddenness of the response but was certainly ready to get this surgery done. I entered an empty office except for the receptionist the next day, then escorted directly into the surgeon's office.

The surgeon proudly displayed his medical credentials framed on the wall. I was suitably impressed. In fact, strangely enough, the surgeon had studied at the university hospital where my mother had undergone historic pacemaker surgery in 1966.

Mother was a medical miracle by giving birth to my precious sister in 1970 as the first woman having had an implanted pacemaker while carrying a child to term and giving birth. While pregnant, Mother underwent surgery to repair a broken wire leading from the pacemaker device to the pericardium, which is the muscle encasing the heart.

My surgeon bounded through the examination room door much different from anything I had imagined. He was a short, chubby, ball of pleasant energy. He wore a wide grin with perfect white teeth, gleaming through a face bronzed from countless hours in the sun. He immediately put me at ease; dressed in tropical garb, sockless loafers and bringing a casual attitude.

First on the list of the patient examination form was a lengthy discussion concerning my surgery, recovery, and complications. He was very concerned but offered no opinions about my condition. The surgeon insisted on pre-surgical testing to ensure that I was stable enough to undergo anesthesia. He also wanted to guarantee that my body would not respond with what could be deadly complications. The physical stress of this simple procedure could result in a sudden stroke or cardiac arrest. Within the week, I had completed the testing. Again, the outcome was not good. However, the need for the port outweighed the possible complications. Still the surgeon refused to take any unnecessary risks and had several specialists standing by in the operating room should the need arise. The greatest concern was my low blood pressure readings.

The lowered blood pressure made administering anesthesia a tricky situation. I would be closely monitored and spend the night in intensive care in case life saving steps were called for.

Two tiny incisions in the left subclavian area just beneath my collarbone allowed the implant of a Groshong Catheter Port. Harpoon season on my fragile veins had finally ended. Though I have never actually seen what the port looks like, when touched through the skin it feels like a small hard disc with little more than a threadlike line running through a vein to my heart. The port allowed infusions of fluid, medication, artificial feedings, blood withdrawal and transfusions. What surprised me most is the lack of experience so many nurses have at accessing the port. Obviously, few nurses are able to access the port even though it's a common medical aid.

As March 2004 arrived, the month marked two years since my gastric by-pass surgery. Again, we were glad to see the milestone because it meant I had survived yet another year. My health was still deteriorating for a variety of reasons. My body weight continued to be unstable. Kidney stones were still the norm. Vomiting was a daily thing. My bowels were never normal. I experienced diarrhea then medication for this led to impaction, likewise medication to clear a blockage led to diarrhea. I experienced nearly constant pain throughout the day.

I was losing my teeth, my bones were brittle and easily broken, malabsorption left my body with serious deficiencies of proper vitamins, nutrients, and minerals. Low blood sugar was the result of the diet I was forced to live with. I continued to tolerate only very soft foods. Solid food was impossible for me; with hope, the situation will eventually be resolved. The very same awful complications still plagued my very existence. Deflated skin hung from my body including my breasts, which were once much larger and fuller. Tears born of frustration came without warning. Would I ever be "normal," at least whatever normal is for a gastric by-pass patient? No one could answer that question.

We met with my university surgeon in April 2004. It was evident at this point that something had to change. We discussed the two basic options with my surgeon. First, an attempt to repair the original surgery and the other option involved a complete reversal of the roux en-y gastric by-pass. He counseled us this surgery could be as serious, if not more so, than the original procedure. When coupled with the complications, my physical state and problems revealed during the surgery itself, this procedure could be, in fact, extremely dangerous or possibly fatal for me.

My university surgeon made it abundantly clear, he was only in favor of doing a complete reversal surgery. He felt if we were going to chance the surgery at all, in view of my present condition, that a reversal was the only option. His reasoning was, due to the continued downward spiral of my condition, much more than my health was threatened. My life was at risk.

The surgeon explained my health had not been stable in the two years since the surgery, therefore, my body had never had a period to adjust to the changes brought on by the surgery. He was extremely concerned with my ability to survive the surgery at all but he did agree that something had to be done and soon. He cautioned us that even with a reversal, my condition might not improve. My university surgeon sent me home to think this over and decide what I wanted to do. I was to email him my decision as soon as possible. He preferred that we make a decision within the course of the next week.

As we walked away from the medical building, I became more upset with every step I took. Silently, we began the two-hour trip home. We stopped for dinner along the way and still didn't speak. I moved my food around on the plate but ate nothing. I was feeling nauseous and depressed. We were on our way again as darkness enveloped the interior of our vehicle. There in the dark, only the sound of my sobs broke the silence.

Chapter Thirteen

~ FEARS OF GOING UNDER
THE KNIFE – AGAIN ~

I blindly gazed into the darkness as we traveled the road home. Tears left damp stains down the length of my cheeks. So many conflicting issues swirled through my brain. I was mute with fear and praying that we'd make the right decision this time. Obviously, my previous choice to have the gastric by-pass was a dismal mistake. Self-loathing tore at my heart for putting my family and friends through this awful myriad of devastating medical complications. The enormous blame of my situation crushed my heart and inundated my conscientiousness with the power of an avalanche. I could put none of this into an intelligible statement, even in my own mind.

Gut-wrenching sobs emanating from my heaving chest troubled my husband much more than the verdict handed down from my university surgeon. Yet he drove without speaking as he patiently waited for me to broach the subject. Until then he quietly respected my silence. He knew when I was ready we'd discus the options laid before us. This was not a decision I had to face alone, but it didn't feel that way now. I was uneasy over the doctor's report. Overwhelmed, I didn't know where to start to determine just how I felt about the options and making peace with it.

Finally, with unsteady composure, I broke the silent barrier. When we first discussed my options over a year ago, he'd given me only two options to regain some small measure of health. A repair or reversal surgery. It seemed as if he was removing the choice to attempt a repair of the original surgery from the negotiation. I trusted my doctor and knew he had my best interest at heart. If I consented to a reversal surgery, all of the heartbreaking agony would have been for naught. I would more than likely regain every pound lost and then some. There was no guarantee a reversal wouldn't leave me with even more health issues than we currently faced and suddenly the fear at going through any surgery at all terrified me. Facing the realities, I did not want to die trying to remain thin. A thin corpse was not my objective.

Another thought gnawed at my very core. I was at fault in this situation. The roux en-y gastric by-pass was elective surgery. I had chosen to do this to myself and now it could very well cost me everything I held dear … even my life. I made the choice to have the surgery primarily because I wanted to be a "normal" weight. That was the bottom line. I did this for vanity, not for the glorious "health reasons" that everyone spouts when trying to justify this surgery to themselves and their families.

Many people, much larger than me, have elected to undergo this surgery to save their lives consumed by fat. I'm keenly familiar with that aspect and can truly sympathize, however, that was not true in my case. I hated the fact I had trouble tying my own shoes or doing anything that required I bend over. To be quite gross, wiping my own butt had been difficult. I wanted to be able to turn over in bed and not feel like I was suffocating while lying on my back. My ankles and knees ached terribly, making it hard to walk or stand for any length of time. I wanted to look nice and to appeal to my husband.

Amazingly, what I failed to understand, I was the only one in our marriage who couldn't accept the extra weight. My husband never saw me as an obese person, he saw only the woman he loved. All of these realizations stood glaring at me. I was thin, stick thin, but reversal surgery would almost certainly bring an end to that. Was I prepared to die for vanity sake?

Terror filled my entire being at the thought of going under the knife once again. It seemed that with each subsequent procedure that required anesthesia, I was gambling with my life. Would I wake up this time? My mind silently screamed in pure panic, I do not want to die! That was the bottom line. I prayed for a "normal" life, to be able to enjoy life again. I could number the "good" days I had experienced the past two years on the fingers of one hand. There were long stretches of time I couldn't remember at all through the thick veil of agony and the drug-induced haze. Those oblivious days, weeks, months were forever past, lost memories never recalled. My choices, thin and dead, or fat and alive; is there a choice? Simply, I choose life. No physical attribute is worth a life. I choose to live.

The only three people I discussed this with were my husband, my sister, and my best friend. Again, my sons should've been included, but being their mother, I continued to protect them from the harsh realities of my situation. I couldn't find it within myself to bring this additional pain and worry to them. The consensus of the people I did include in the decision was that they wanted me to be alive, healthy, and happy, nothing more, in that order. Fat or thin did not make me any more or less dear to any of them. Those that love me continually reminded me I wasn't at fault here. I had faced all of this as informed and prepared as possible.

The other extenuating circumstance that came to mind was that our youngest son would soon graduate high school. His education had been a long, hard fought process due to his handicap. I would not miss it, his special day, not under any circumstances. I might arrive strapped to a gurney, trailing an IV but I would be there. This fact was not up for discussion. God willing, I would watch my son receive his diploma.

After extensive discussions and pondering all aspects of what ifs, the conclusion was that I wanted the surgeon to try to repair the gastric by-pass. Therefore, I set out to convince him to try. If repair proved impossible, then I would accept the fact that a reversal was required to save my life. I prayed that my surgeon would agree. I had complete faith in him and his treatment decisions. I knew beyond a doubt I'd have to trust his surgical skills and judgment. Because of the original gastric by-pass surgery, trusting a surgeon was probably one of the largest obstacles I faced.

I composed a heartfelt and carefully worded email, honestly relating all of my feelings to my university surgeon. Carefully, I detailed each of my concerns in hopes he'd understand. To my amazement, he responded saying he was willing to make a deal with me. He would enter the surgical suite with the intention of repairing the surgery; however, if he saw this was not likely to better my condition, he would reverse the surgery. If he felt the only alternative was to do a reversal, he'd notify my husband during the surgery and allow him to make the decision to leave things as they were or proceed. I could ask no more of him. I placed my life in his very capable hands. I was strangely calmed by the final decision.

Wasting no time, the surgery would take place in two weeks. I was admitted into the hospital immediately so that my body could be built up as much as possible to withstand the surgery. The doctor closely guarded against all complications, if this procedure had any chance to succeed. I was on a regime of massive vitamins, three protein drinks a day through my feeding tube, and intensive antibiotics. Secluded in a completely germ free environment, everyone who saw me had to dress from head to foot in yellow hospital garb. Everyone looked like Big Bird!

My husband hired a cleaning crew to sterilize our house so that when I came home from the hospital it would be germ-free. After surgery, my restriction to the house was extremely limited. Anyone visiting me had to be free of illness within the past thirty days. Even if healthy, everyone coming in from the outside must wear full gown, gloves, mask, hair, and shoe covers. It was going to be a very difficult time to endure for all of us, but we had no choice.

As the date quickly approached, I became more and more unsettled. I hadn't changed my mind in any way but quite simply, I was afraid. I described the feelings to my surgeon, who understood completely. He assured me these feelings were entirely normal for anyone facing surgery, especially given my experience over the past two years.

My dear surgeon offered to give me something to help settle my nerves. He sympathetically assured me that none of the problems I faced were a product of my imagination, of hypochondria, or any type of psychosis. The health issues were truly beyond my control. Yet, I still bore the mental and emotional scars inflicted upon me by my initial surgeon. When properly cared for, my university surgeon's assurance and concern brought me to tears. Nothing about my health situation was, or had ever been, psychosomatic.

The "date with destiny" arrived. My husband, younger son, sister and dad were there for me looking like fuzzy Easter chicks in their yellow head to toe sanitary cover-ups. I had held out hope that the surgeon could do the surgery laparoscopically so I could avoid even more surgical scars already crisscrossing my belly like a road map. He informed me open surgery was necessary, meaning I would have another three-inch incision, so nothing would interfere with his view. On the upside, he promised to try to utilize a site already scarred. The surgery would last approximately two hours with an additional hour for recovery.

Surgery preparation began, we met with the anesthesiologist and then my surgeon came in to speak to us. My husband kissed me sweetly and then away we went to the frigid operating room. Heated blankets swaddling around me eased the chill when the operating room nurse noticed I was shivering. The monitors began beeping with the rhythm of my heart, which was thumping as if might leap from my chest. The anesthesiologist gently whispered to me he was about to inject medication in my IV, then I would feel a little drowsy. Immediately oblivion overtook my senses and I remembered nothing further.

I awoke later in recovery feeling the sting of the incision in my belly with no idea of how much time had actually elapsed. I was anxious to know the results, but the nurses refused to tell me. Their response made me just that much more anxious. Had the surgery reversed? What did he find? I wanted to know the results yet I feared the outcome. My husband was soon by my side and said he'd spoken with the doctor but the only details he knew were that things had gone as well as expected. Now, I was truly afraid.

The time seemed to drag by as I watched every tick of the

clock. The surgeon came in for the long awaited report. I suddenly realized I was holding my breath in anticipation of the answers to come. I concentrated on simply breathing and felt as if I was about to hyperventilate.

The problems were extensive. First, my intestine was kinked or strangulated in three places. The intestine had been pulled up tight behind and over the top of the old stomach then reconnected to the backside of what was thought to be my stomach pouch. The lower intestinal Y-connection was also strangulated due to the intestine connection. He repaired a hernia in my bowel and nearly five pounds of scar tissue was cut away.

The scar tissue left serious adhesions and had attached itself to several major organs including the suspected stomach pouch, liver, bladder, and left kidney. The section my doctor had assumed was a tiny stomach pouch, scar tissue had it tightly fisted. According to the doctor, if indeed it were a pouch, it was virtually useless to me now or in the future. The surgeon, along with several other highly acclaimed university gastroenterologists, called in to confer during the course of the operation, agreed it didn't appear a stomach pouch even existed, therefore, the doctor did a biopsy to confirm their suspicions. We'd know for sure the next day when the results were complete. The surgeon repaired what he could, though he said there was very little to work with that remained undamaged. In his professional opinion, a reversal surgery was not possible under any circumstance.

According to my university surgeon, circumstances were that my system would never be "normal" again. After he finally obtained surgical notes from the original hospital, the notes revealed the amputation of six feet of my intestine. Malabsorption would be a problem for me the remainder of my life. The first few feet of the intestine is the area where all calories, vitamins, and nutrients are absorbed into the body from food intake. This is also where medication is broken down to take effect.

The "standard *roux-en-y* surgery" calls for the removal of two feet of intestine. The stomach pouch, which again for "standard surgery", is generally one to two ounces. We'd soon find out if I had any sort of pouch at all. Nothing could be done to change my situation, my body would never heal. We could only hope my health would stabilize.

My university surgeon stated that, at best, the original surgery performed was an intensive gastric by-pass surgery. However, he wouldn't comment further except to say the surgery was "not routinely done." The extensive surgery I had was more appropriate for someone twice my size or well over five hundred pounds. We knew to a certain extent, physicians banded together, one would usually never criticize another surgeon. My university surgeon adhered to this unwritten oath.

Radiologists, it seems, are not bound to the same sense of brotherhood banding together. The next morning the head of the radiology department at the university hospital came into my room and informed us my surgery appeared to have been a "hack job." Though my university surgeon couldn't promise me anything concrete, he felt I'd get some relief from my symptoms because of the minimal repair. Only time would tell.

Five weeks after surgery, I watched with great pride as my baby boy graduated from high school. I pushed through the pain all day and only faltered slightly. I managed to stand on my own two feet and make it through the day. We (our family) hosted a Senior Breakfast for his small graduating class and the faces of those kids made my struggles seem non-existent. As I watched my son receive his diploma, emotion filled my heart, this is what I live for. This child, his brother, my husband, family, friends, all of those people who have offered my name up in prayer. I have a life worth living, worth fighting for. God, give me the strength to go on, I prayed.

Chapter Fourteen

~ *A ROCKY ROAD TO RECOVERY* ~

I spent ten days in the hospital following surgery, and then the real recovery time began, without nurses and intravenous pain medicine. Recovery was harder on me physically this go-round. My diminished physical strength and nearly non-existent immunities made the process tedious. I struggled to regain waning energy by forcing myself to be a little more active every day. By early afternoon, I was napping like a kindergartner and by 8:30 p.m., I was down for the night.

I began to feel somewhat better when kidney stones landed me in the emergency room again. IV fluids had flushed the stones through my urinary system. In a feeble attempt to make light of the situation, through the pain, I began asking nurses if they wanted their urine samples "on the rocks." My little joke met with a questioning stare as if to say, "What in world is she talking about?" The nurses probably thought I was delirious.

No adjective comes close when describing the blinding pain of kidney stones. I know I'm repeating myself here but unless you've experienced them you could never imagine the shear hell of passing these stones. Miraculously, after two years of constant misery, I had grown accustomed to the excruciating torment of the malady. The affliction, known to bring a grown man literally to his knees and beg for his mother, would attack without warning. What I felt now began as a nagging ache in my lower back, followed by a soaring fever. If the stones were small, they would pass at home without medical attention.

This particular episode proved to be quite serious. When my urologist read the X-rays, he determined the right kidney had numerous stones. The size of these stones guaranteed I would never be able to pass them, therefore, they required immediate attention. He recommended extensive outpatient work on the right kidney, using several different procedures in order to clear as many stones as possible. The urologist planned to insert a stint to widen the ureter, allowing the stones to pass with less discomfort. The stint would remain in place for approximately two weeks. We'd been down this road before, it had become nearly routine.

Luckily, the doctor would do the procedures under general anesthesia, which is always a good thing when pain is involved. When the procedures were complete, the urologist had removed twenty-four stones using a "surgical basket." Then the urologist shattered many of the remaining stones using lithotripsy. That procedure involves a focused, high-intensity shock wave, applied externally while the patient lies on a water-filled device to protect the area of concentration. The shock waves, administered in time with the patient's heartbeat, steadily increase in intensity. The doctor must use extreme caution. If the shock waves grow too forceful, the patient will awaken from the anesthesia and be in incredible pain. After coming out of anesthesia from the hour-long procedure, I felt weakened and sore. Six days passed before I felt any relief at all.

By the time two weeks passed, I actually felt good for a change. Our youngest son and I decided after my appointment with the urologist to remove the stint, we'd do a little shopping. I was so happy to be doing "normal" everyday things. I was actually excited in anticipation of our trip to Wal-Mart.

I knew what to expect involving the stint removal, after all, I had removed the last one myself. The mood was light in the doctor's office as the doctor and his nurse casually chatted about the process. The nurse mentioned she'd never seen or removed a stint and within moments it was determined this would be her first introduction to the process. I was a little nervous, what could possibly happen? She prepped me, then gave the string a firm tug and out came the stint. One sudden twinge of pain then it was all over. They left the room, I dressed and was on my way. The doctor's visit was as simple as that. I had no way of knowing that within twenty-four hours, I would be near death.

My youngest son and I ran a few errands before going home that afternoon. Once we returned home, I realized I was exhausted. I lay down for a quick nap, but slept for the remainder of the afternoon. After preparing a simple supper, I returned to bed and slept through the night.

My husband was off to work very early. I hadn't even heard him stir that morning. Once I awoke, I realized something was very wrong. My skin was fiery to the touch, dizziness left me unsteady as I tried to sit on the edge of the bed. My vision refused to focus. I rose to my feet but my legs buckled beneath me. Stunned, I fell to the floor. I called out to my son who was staying with us for a time. "Call Dad," I shouted to him.

I couldn't make sense out of what was happening to me. My son was frantic. Did we need an ambulance? Call Dad, call Dad. It would take my husband thirty minutes to get to me. My son was concerned that waiting was too risky. He was terrified, but my husband thought he was overreacting.

My son's girlfriend called my urologist whose nurse insisted I take Tylenol to relieve the fever and drink plenty of water to rehydrate. They weren't taking the situation seriously. The doctor was in surgery that morning so we would have to wait until he was available.

Once my husband arrived, he knew immediately I was in desperate trouble. I needed medical attention at once. The thermometer read one hundred four degrees. I faded in and out of consciousness. My husband called the urologist's office. Instructed to come to the large hospital to the north of us by way of the emergency room as soon as possible, medical orders would await us there. My husband tried to help me dress. It was a losing battle. By this time I was no longer conscious. He did manage to get a shirt and pair of sweat pants on me, then lifted me into his arms and carried me to the truck. He broke every speeding law on the books, trying to get me to the hospital. At this point, he began to fear for my life. I can recall none of this. Instead, I refer to my husbands' carefully kept notes and my son's memories to fill the gaps.

My fever continued to soar, now one hundred five degrees. The nurse recorded my blood pressure was slipping dangerously low as I struggled to remain conscious . Terrified, my senses seemed to spin as sights and sounds swarmed about, I could not seem to focus. I had no idea what was happening to me. The emergency room attending nurse called my urologist again to inform him of my steadily deteriorating condition. He left instructions again, Tylenol would bring down the fever. It was obvious to all of the medical personnel who tended me, my life was in serious danger at this point. My urologist left a message he'd see me in his office the following morning, further informing the nurse she could leave any testing results to be gone through at that time. He was treating me for a urinary tract infection and felt any additional issues could be addressed at the office visit.

Rather than stabilize, my condition continued to worsen. The emergency room nurse was growing increasingly concerned. He called the urologist a third time. The doctor was beginning to get more and more irritated over the whole situation. Finally, the decision was that I stay in the hospital for overnight observation but still nothing more serious than an infection resulting from repeated kidney stones was suspected. The thermometer continued to read higher, more dangerous numbers, my blood pressure refused to register at all. I slipped into shock and my life was fading.

As I was settled into the hospital bed, a nurse rushed into the room with paperwork moving me into the Intensive Care Unit (ICU). I went to the unit without explanation and suddenly I was afraid. My husband was deeply concerned as well, but true to form, he did not voice it. What was wrong with me? Where was my doctor? I needed to see my regular physician. I hadn't as yet seen any doctor. What was happening? Intensive Care meant this current complication was much more serious than we were lead to believe. My condition continued to decline steadily yet the doctor gave no additional orders beyond Tylenol to treat the fever. Without further orders from the attending physician, no additional medication could be given.

Once in the ICU, a man in green surgical scrubs walked up and casually picked up my chart. It appeared his interest was more out of curiosity than medical consultation. I had no idea who this man was but as he read the chart, he would glance over at me. His face seemed to grow more flushed with every glimpse. He may have introduced himself, but nothing he said registered with me. He immediately dismissed my husband to the waiting room. Abruptly, my husband was informed that someone would be out to speak to him as soon as possible and with that the door was closed in his face. Hours later, my husband was told this doctor was the physician in charge of the ICU.

The doctor belted out orders at the top of his lungs. Apparently, I was in toxic shock and my entire system had gone septic. Those were the only words my husband heard as he stood horrified at the ICU door. The doctor issued commands for testing, medications, IV's and for someone to get my attending physician on the phone immediately. The nurses moved at lightening speed to carry out the doctor's orders. It was very hard to keep up with the constant motion. Still in shock, I was slipping in and out of consciousness. A nurse questioned one of the doctor's mandates. He immediately banned her from the unit with the statement, "If you're not here to help, get out of my way."

The gruff, demanding doctor spoke very softly and sweetly in my ear saying he was doing everything he could to make things better for me. Further, that he had to get lines in me, my veins had collapsed, so what he was about to do was going to hurt like hell (those were his very words) but he'd try to get it over with quickly then give me something for the pain. It didn't occur to me to ask why I couldn't have pain medication before the procedure if it was going to hurt so badly. We were later told that my blood pressure had been so low that until I was stabilized, pain medication would only make the situation worse. I was very close to cardiac arrest.

The doctor made a three-inch incision and two smaller

incisions on each side of my inner thighs. I screamed in pain as the scalpel sliced through my skin. I saw blood spurt in an arc and begin to pool beneath me. I felt the world shift as darkness began to envelop me. My arms and legs were held firmly in restraints. I tightly clenched my fists, fingernails digging into my palms. Blood soon dyed the pristine white sheets a sticky red. I prayed this hell would soon be over. The nurse at my head tried to calm me as I cried out in pain, ; stroking my hair and speaking in reassuring whispers in my ear. The doctor then made an incision in my neck to thread a line into my carotid artery. My mind could no longer take the intensive pain as I held my body tight against the doctor's sharp knife. I felt the puncture of a wire probing my neck. Then darkness gratefully claimed me.

As the ICU doctor spoke to my husband, the phone rang and, of course, it was for him. Everyone standing within earshot could hear his side of the conversation as he began to raise his voice immediately. In fact, it was my urologist's partner, who was on call this particular night. He was returning the physician's urgent call, yet there was a different take on the gravity of my situation. The doctor explained, and not in a calm voice, I needed to go into surgery within the hour. The physician shouted into the telephone, "Doctor, I'm not asking you to attend to your patient, I'm telling you without surgery she won't see morning." Without waiting for a response, he slammed down the phone.

The report my husband heard was far from comforting. The physician informed him my system had gone septic, a disease had invaded my blood, my organs were in trauma and had begun shutting down. He left my husband with the words he was trying everything he knew how to do to save my life. My husband walked into the waiting room in a blind daze, trying to figure out what to do next. The nurse poked her head out of the unit and let him know I was going into emergency surgery within the next ten minutes. The physician would speak to him further when possible.

My husband's only response was "please save her." He was horror stricken, refusing to believe I wouldn't survive. We lived with the belief that as long as there was life, there was hope. Not knowing what else to do in this situation, my husband left the waiting room for the smoking area to determine his next move and call everyone on our notification list. What would he say to our children, our families? He began calling but saved the last, most difficult calls until the end.

Repeatedly summoned over the hospital speaker system, my husband was oblivious to the announcement. The nurses were frantically trying to have him return to ICU. Outside in the hot, sticky July night, he failed to hear the emergency call. As he nervously passed the time among the other people congregated in the garage area, someone over heard him speaking and asked if he was with the Goddard family. When he nodded in reply, the stranger reported that the nurses were looking for him everywhere upstairs.

My poor husband bolted in a panicked run for the hospital entrance and the elevator. Sheer terror coursed through his body and sweat soaked his shirt. Visibly shaken, a shudder of adrenaline worked its way down his spine, his heart beating so loudly he could hardly think. Willing himself not to imagine the worst, he silently prayed standing there alone in the elevator. "Please God, don't take her from me."

When he arrived at the nurses' station, he was asked to sign paperwork to allow "life sustaining" devices to be implemented including a heart/lung machine, respirator, blood transfusions and kidney dialysis. Without thinking, he signed the papers put before him, he only wanted to see me alive. As tears filled his eyes, the lump in his throat threatened to close his airway. He mentally squared his shoulders and refused to give in to panic. The nurses advised my husband to remain in the waiting room, as soon as the doctor was out of surgery, he would want a consultation. He returned to the waiting room, his body and mind numb, and then slumped in a chair to begin the horrible wait and worry.

His sister arrived to wait with him. My sister, Dad and a cousin arrived to sit the vigil as well. Soon the ICU waiting room filled with people all praying for me. It was to be a long wait as more than six hours ticked away until the summons to the nurses' station came. Everyone sat on the edge of their seats for the news.

The ICU doctor agreed to speak to everyone so the story would not have to be repeated multiple times. He described my condition as stable but extremely critical. I had come through the surgery alive ... my survival would be from hour to hour at this point. The ICU physician said he would be staying by my side until I was out of danger.

In a lighter voice, the doctor reported he had me on every antibiotic he could spell. With any luck my useless kidneys would rebound, stints were again in place to ease the stress on the ill-used organs. I was in recovery. Only my husband and children could see me, possibly within the hour.

The hour time frame came and went. The second hour passed and still there was no call allowing entry into the inner sanctum of ICU. Unable to withstand the pressure, my husband pressed the buzzer outside the unit. A nurse answered the call, she asked him to remain patient. He couldn't see me until my condition had stabilized. Stabilized? He thought I had stabilized after surgery. Now, filled with nervous energy, he paced the length and width of the small waiting room.

The delay worried him. He needed to see me, needed to watch my chest rise and fall, if for no other reason than to be reassured I was still alive. Finally, the nurse called his name. At this point only two people could come see me for five minutes. My husband and his sister were first to approach the door. Given gowns, gloves, mask, hair and shoe covers, they were warned not touch me. Neither was prepared for what they saw when they entered the glassed cubicle with a nurse constantly at my side monitoring every beat of my heart.

Testing found a blood-born bacteria had brought me to the brink of death. The scene that met my husband was much worse then he had imagined. My body was bloated due to low kidney function, a respirator crept down my throat to assist my breathing, a naso-gastric tube snaked into my nasal passage, my legs were in stirrups with four lines running from each femoral artery, catheters everywhere imaginable, and a central line in my carotid artery ported four more lines. Bags hung all around me, totaling fifteen lines feeding my body with medication. Each line taped to a tongue depressor along the bedside railings identifying the particular medication being pushed through each line. A catheter in my bladder helped drain the poisoned fluids from my body. Another central line in my arm sent doses of pain medication to keep me sedated in a drugged-induced coma.

The constant beeping of the heart-lung machine broke the still silence. The ventilator made swooshing sounds forcing oxygen into my airway. Another machine monitored my vital signs every three minutes. Still another in the tall cabinet by my side measured the oxygen in my blood. I lay on a bed with a mattress filled with air that recorded my weight and temperature continually. A soft cushioned "egg-crate" was stretched out beneath me to protect my body from bed-sores that are all too common in patients who are unable to move or turn for a considerable length of time. The primary diagnosis was methicillin-resistant staphylococcus aureus, commonly called MRSA. The highly contagious infection compromised my body to a point where it had no antibodies or immunities to fight illness or disease.

Powerful antibiotics coursed through my veins, which were so strong other bacterial infections often resulted. My condition slowly improved after several harrowing days. Finally, there was reason to hope for my survival. Frayed nerves of my exhausted family relaxed a little in the waiting room.

Unfortunately, my temperature spiked three days later, plunging my status to critical condition once again. The oxygen levels in my blood refused to stabilize and then my blood pressure descended to life threatening numbers. Frantically, the nurses and doctor worked with me for nine hours straight until my life was no longer in eminent danger. At the nurses shift change, the doctor promised the ICU nurses that he would buy each of them dinner and pay double overtime if they would consent to staying with me for an additional shift. He felt my frail condition mandated continuity. The doctor didn't want a new shift of nurses to care for me until I was completely out of danger. My complications were so massive, a nursing staff unfamiliar with the case could further acerbate my tenuous recovery. Each nurse graciously remained on duty. By morning my condition reached a very unsteady stabilization.

Sometime during the early morning hours, the ICU doctor phoned the hospital pharmacy to request a certain medication. The pharmacy informed him this was not a standard medication carried by the hospital. A special order could take at least forty-eight hours. According to the doctor, that was two days too late. Incensed but not defeated, the doctor commanded one of the ICU nurses to phone all of the local pharmacies until she found the medication. Once located, he reached into his own wallet to pay for the vital medicine.

After testing revealed that my implanted port, which was taken out during surgery as a possible source of the bacterial infection, was negative, it was ruled out as the source of the MRSA. Quite often, medical personnel unintentionally transmit this type of infection to frequently ill or hospitalized patients. Improper sanitation from one patient to the next often rapidly spread the infection. The spread of serious infectious disease, such as life-threatening MRSA, is one of the fundamental reasons hospitals, as well as doctor's offices, have installed bacterial disinfectant stations in each room.

MRSA can be present without any outward symptoms, however, any break in the skin, internal port, catheter, etc. may easily advance the disease as a blood-born infection. Introduced in the blood, the infection can become life-threatening very quickly. The MRSA found to be in my blood had begun to attack the major organs of my body, destroying my immune system.

The doctor adjusted the sedating pain medication that held me in a drug-induced coma. He allowed my family to see me briefly then only for a few fleeting moments. I tried hopelessly to communicate an itch, pain, and nausea. The respirator that assisted my breathing, also prohibited me from speaking. My husband finally brought me a pad and paper.

He has kept these sheets of my first communications to this day. The confused thoughts of my disjointed mind are difficult for us to look at. They bring the entire horrible episode to the forefront of our minds. It was terrifying at how close to death I had come during this time. The first note I frantically wrote described to my husband the horror of blood spurting like a movie special effect when the ICU doctor had cut into the arteries in my legs, "blood everywhere!" was my frightened silent scream. There were numerous pages of my drugged, dazed ramblings. As the powerful pain medication claimed my consciousness, the shaky scrawl sleepily drifted off the page.

The nurses spent several days attempting to wean me off the respirator. At first, I could breathe on my own for two to three minutes. Then exhaustion would overcome me and my breathing became terrified gasps leading to hyperventilation. After working with me for more than a week, I was finally able to breathe on my own. The surgeon removed the awful respirator. I had been on total life support for more than ten days at that point.

The first gulping breath without the tube felt as if it were laced with razors in my throat and made me feel incredible pain. The taste in my mouth was indescribable, gross. With a sore, hoarse voice, I croaked that I desperately wanted to brush my teeth. The nurse brought me a toothbrush with paste and before she could return with water and a basin, I frantically began scrubbing my long-neglected teeth. The group surrounding me giggled with nervous relief.

Eighteen harrowing life-threatening days in ICU passed before relocation to an isolation room was possible. The MRSA left me weakened and immunologically deficient. I was also very contagious, so special precautions were still observed by the medical staff and visitors. My kidneys seemed to have recovered sufficiently enough to warrant the removal of the catheter, for which I was tremendously grateful. Most of the swelling had subsided as well. Still considered to be in serious condition, I was no longer in imminent danger of dying.

I could barely stand the stench of my own body and the greasy feel of my unwashed hair. I pleaded with my husband to clean my body. The lines running into my body from every imaginable angle made a regular sponge bath out of the question but taking pity on me, one of the nurses mercifully wiped me down as best she could. My hair would have to wait. I was so grateful, the effort made me feel so much better.

Five days later, I was happy to move into a regular hospital room. Close attention to avoid any outside germs was mandatory. Once contracting MRSA, the body always carries it and at any given time, the full force of the infection can return with the same devastating complications. Everyone who entered the room continued to don full medical regalia. I finally felt better and was just so happy to be alive.

I went into surgery to have the central line in my carotid artery removed as well as one of the femoral catheters and a new feeding tube implanted. Released from the hospital with strict instructions to stay out of the public, I was very happy to go home. For the next six weeks, I had to undergo daily infusions of two very powerful antibiotics through the remaining femoral catheter in my right leg. In order to tolerate the side effects of these antibiotics, I had to take regular doses of nausea medication much like those of a cancer patient on chemotherapy.

The first thing on my agenda was to wash my hair. The catheter couldn't get wet so a shower or bath was out of the question but I bent over the kitchen sink and with the help of my wonderful husband, we washed my hair. The effort sapped what little strength I had and I fell into an exhausted but contented sleep.

To compound my current situation, it became evident our area was in the direct path of Hurricane Frances. Our neighborhood, nestled between the St. Mary's River and Atlantic Ocean, had to evacuate. My husband hurriedly began to prepare our home for the intense wind, rain and rising waters always present with these storms. The home healthcare nursing staff called, informing us that within the next forty-eight hours I had to evacuate due to my fragile condition. The choices were either hospitalization or evacuation to a location of my choice with nursing care readily available and verified by my doctor before we left.

We decided to retreat to my hometown where I had an abundance of family members. I was very fortunate to have a cousin who was a home healthcare nurse and she was glad to look after me. I am so grateful for the loving care she provided me during this time. Recently, my dear cousin passed her state nursing boards, has found a great job pursuing her dream and decided to go back to school to finish her degree. She did all this while maintaining a household, as well as caring for a husband and three children. She has met with a number of obstacles along the way but handled everyone with grace and dignity. I am extremely proud of her.

My sister's home is some four hours inland so we decided to make this our base of operations. Ironically, as we moved into my sister's home with all of my medical gear, she and her family left for a Caribbean cruise. I thought she was nuts, talk about sailing into the eye of the storm. The cruise line assured all of us (I called to check for myself) they could easily avoid the weather by changing their ports of call. Off they went and we moved into her house.

We maintained a constant vigil around the TV weather channel, noting every small movement of the hurricane. My delighted family celebrated having us in their midst and hosted several cookouts to visit with us. I was not very strong and still plagued with constant nausea. My husband diligently managed my visitation schedule and I spent the majority of the time sleeping.

Routine nursing care involved cleaning the site of the femoral central line. My husband, who is very well-trained, administered the regular doses of antibiotics, supplemental feedings and fluids, so this process was not a problem. Then unexpectedly, I developed a high fever late one night. My cousin rushed to my side to evaluate the problem. The skin around the central line had become suddenly red and angry. The site began to drain a foul-smelling, thick greenish secretion. Obviously, the central line was infected.

My hometown is very small with only a very limited hospital facility. We were certain that if I were to go to the emergency room, medical personnel would immediately want to ship me off in an ambulance to a larger more well-equipped hospital fifty miles to the north. That would be fifty miles further away from our home to doctors who knew nothing of my case. The thought of dealing with another set of doctors, going through all of my medical history, extensive testing and so forth was unthinkable.

Because a good number of the telephone lines were down, getting in touch with our family doctor was nearly impossible. After hours of frustration, calling and redialing, we finally were able to connect with his phone service. Late the next evening, we were extremely relieved to hear his voice on the other end of the phone line. He advised that when an all clear announcement posted, I should get to our local hospital. If a red line appeared on my leg from the wound or Tylenol failed to lower the fever, we were to call 911 and have them dispatch an ambulance immediately. No exceptions.

Three days later, we headed home to survey the damage that awaited us. By the time the weather broke, we had just enough time to make our way home. We were grateful to find little damage other than a missing trashcan and piles of debris in the yard. My right leg had begun to swell to enormous proportions, feeling as though it might burst and looked a scarlet red in color. I could barely lift the appendage. When I walked, I had to drag it. I was unable to bend or put any weight on it at all. I was truly terrified. What was happening to me now?

Two more hurricanes, Ivan and Jeanne, gathered strength in the Atlantic threatening to batter the southeastern coast. I had no choice at this point—admission into our local hospital. A MRI showed a very serious blood clot beneath the central line in my right leg. Blood tests showed the flare up of the MRSA. I was again in seriously guarded condition. Again, a call went out to our family that for the second time in as many months, my life was threatened. Tremendously scared, I alternated between tears and prayer.

My condition worsened. My family doctor and university surgeon had conferred and left me no choice. In the pouring rain, a screaming ambulance moved me from our local hospital to the large university facility. Heavily sedated, the trip entailed as little trauma during the transfer as possible. My husband and son followed the ambulance on our southward trek as the rest of the traffic headed north, away from the impending tropical hurricanes.

Once settled, visitation was restricted. Due to my situation, the doctor relegated me to an isolation room away from any further potential hazards. Then my body rejected the feeding tube, which provided all of the nutrients that I consumed. An infection in my mouth made it impossible for me to take in anything orally.

I felt my stomach suck in the feeding tube and then release, it felt like a bobber pulled underwater then released to soar to the surface. It was an eerie sensation but also very painful. When applied, pressure to the tender tissue of my belly and the incision around the feeding tube burned and ached with nearly constant pain. Due to precarious health concerns, abnormal anatomical makeup and further complications of infection as well as the blood clot, it was determined I should be moved to the special care ward of the university hospital.

I had a nurse of my own. Again, limited visitation and then they were required to don the Big Bird outfits for only twenty minutes every four hours. The strong, abusive antibiotics made me feel worse than the actual condition. My grossly swollen leg and toes looked as though they might explode. The whole leg throbbed in agony making my attempts to relax impossible.

Again into surgery, the surgeon replaced the feeding tube and the femoral central line was removed. Under close examination, an attempt to dissolve the blood clot failed to have any effect. The clot made my condition critical. I was in danger of it breaking away and traveling to my heart, lungs or brain causing a heart attack, stroke or embolism. If the clot continued to grow, it could totally block the artery and it was possible that I could lose my leg. The doctor ordered massive blood thinners and I was put on complete bed rest until my condition stabilized. I was not even allowed out of bed to go to the bathroom.

I was in pain, lonely, worried about my family, pets and home with the hurricanes growing ever closer. My husband and son were in a hotel near the hospital, coming in to see me whenever the hospital staff would allow. Our oldest son decided to remain in his apartment, though the city had issued a voluntary evacuation. He is young and felt invincible. Being Mom, I worried for his safety but since he is an adult, I had to accept his decision to stay home. Still, I made him promise to check in regularly. I prayed we wouldn't lose telephone service. To lessen some of my worry, he traveled to our home, picking up the dog and cat to keep them safe from harm.

The entire medical staff was instructed to report to the hospital with extra clothing, all essentials and sleeping bags. The staff was to remain on duty for the duration until danger of the hurricanes had passed. No patients were to be released until the local authorities issued an all clear notice.

The worst of the weather pummeled the area during the wee hours of the morning. No one in the hospital slept without chemical inducement. From the window, which the hospital barricaded, you could see huge trees bending to the ground with the massive force of the wind. The windows actually flexed from the interior pressure. Tree branch missiles and debris flew through the air. The hospital maintenance staff battened down everything possible. Road signs were dislodged. Like anything loosened by the ferocious wind, they dangerously took flight. The hospital operated on auxiliary power generators, the remainder of the town dark with no power at all.

Ironically, the hurricane hit the university town with much more force than we would have experienced at home. Many of the hospital windows were shattered and the first floor flooded. Power came on some twelve hours later and my husband said that downstairs, the carpet squished when you walked across the floor. The staff busily cleaned everything to avoid the health risks of disease carrying mildew and mold.

Two days after the hurricanes passed, the doctor allowed me to go home under the strict supervision of the home healthcare nurses who would stay with me continually for a week. After that initial period, the nurses could decrease their visits to twice daily for several weeks following. I was going from the isolation of the hospital to house arrest, but at least I was going home.

The trip home was like viewing a battle zone and many detours extended the trip to avoid downed power lines. Uprooted trees littered the roadside, debris hung from trees, roofs torn away and water flowed through the ditches and streets. Thankfully, no casualties resulted in our area. The most horrible devastation was much further south. We were fortunate to have only seen the remnants of the killer hurricanes. Our home withstood the worst of the weather and everything was fine. A few downed branches in the yard and leaves everywhere but that was the extent of it, we were so very fortunate.

The mail had stacked up in our absence and as I flipped through it, I noticed a letter from the Office of Personnel Management. I held the letter, afraid to break the seal. Like ripping off a Band-Aid, I tore off the end of the envelope and noticed I was holding my breath. My medical retirement had been approved. I was now officially retired. Even though this was the best possible outcome for me, I was sad my career was at an end. The government declared me totally disabled, which was just another loss to add to the devastation of gastric by-pass surgery. I might have dealt better with this situation had the idea to retire at forty-two been mine but because I had no choice in the matter, it left me feeling troubled.

The toll of my botched surgery continued to rise. I was thankful I still had my writing, but I loved the people I worked with and hated the forced separation. What would I do now? How would we survive without my paycheck? Financially, we were so far behind we were in danger of losing our home. Medical bills, after my insurance had paid, now ballooned to more than $500,000.00. The surgery had cost us financial stability as well. Guilt surged through me. I had never wanted any of this to happen. I had only prayed for a better life. I had prayed the surgery would change my life, but not like this.

Chapter Fifteen

~ *FEEDING TUBES* ~

Once it was safe for me to venture out into public again, I faced the task of cleaning out my office then through the checkout process at work. I put off the arduous tasks as long as I reasonably could. I didn't want to say "goodbye" to the guys. This meant closing a very important chapter in my life so I avoided the inevitable. My ultimate goal was to one day be able to support myself writing and leave my "real" job. However, I wanted it to be my decision when to take this important step. Our family would have to be financially stable enough for me to do so. My career was now stripped away from me and I had absolutely no choice in the matter.

Physically, I knew I was unable to return to work. Constantly in and out of the hospital, passing kidney stones weekly, the blood clot, nausea and vomiting every day, constipation and diarrhea made for a full life on its own. I always seemed to be exhausted and there were days when I could barely get off the couch to tend my own personal needs. I continued to receive feedings and antibiotics everyday, fluid infusions each week. My port had malfunctioned so it became necessary to change out the device. Now I had matching scars on both sides of my chest.

How did I expect to return to work when I never knew what condition I would wake up to each morning? One moment, I'd feel fine then the next I might be in the midst of plunging sugar, vomiting uncontrollably or indescribable pain, literally bringing me to my knees. Fluctuating sugar brought on because of my limited diet was a deadly complication. Most of the soft foods I was able to consume were largely carbohydrate, which metabolizes into digestive sugar causing my blood sugar numbers to soar upward then plummet to the lowest depths humanly tolerated. In fact, during a follow-up exam at the university doctor's office, when checked, my sugar was at an all time low of thirty-two. Normal numbers are considered between eighty and one hundred. The doctor was shocked, very concerned I was about to pass out. As my body began to sweat profusely, I felt chilled to the bone, accompanied by a total inability to concentrate or focus my vision. Tremors gripped my limbs and my hands were often unable to manage my sugar-monitoring machine or pour myself a simple glass of juice to way-lay the ugly symptoms. My feet and hands would often tingle and grow numb. To top it all off, I would sometimes be temporarily blinded.

Nausea and convulsions often heaved through my abdomen and threatened to crush my ribs as I retched in whatever vessel was near my hands. I felt many times as if my inner organs would rip from my body and spew from my throat as the unproductive spasms contorted my every muscle. Grossly, I have found myself retching into the trashcan as diarrhea wrung out my already dehydrated system. The process left me weak, quivering in pain and exhausted. I know this story of my complications sounds redundant, but again "welcome to my world."

Sometimes one or more of these conditions describe a day in my life. The pain of passing a stone leads to nausea or imbalanced sugar leads to nausea. One state of being brings on such torment that my sensibilities are overwhelmed and all I can do is rock my body, sobbing. My initial surgeon said my symptoms were unreal and that I was psychotic. Well, a body can only go through so much. Eventually, I've questioned my own sanity. All I could do is pray I'll get through this moment, this hour, this day. Then pray this repeated torture will not end my life. Some time in this weakened and pain-riddled brain, I prayed for death to end the constant anguish.

Finally, I recovered enough from the current episode to

make my way to the office. Tears streamed down my cheeks as I cleaned out my desk. Ending this chapter of my life was probably one of the hardest things I have ever done. As I packed away fifteen years, I knew a new day was dawning for me and that was the only way I would get through the process. The guys took me to lunch for a final farewell. Once we returned to the office, I was too exhausted to complete the checkout procedure. I let my now former supervisor know I'd have to return another day to finish. I've never gone back. In a way, I guess it's just a stubborn way of holding on to that last crumb of my professional life. I met with the guys several times in the following months but our lives have taken different turns and many of them have since retired.

During the late summer, August and September, my feeding tube began to cause me a great deal of discomfort once more. It would pull inward with great force, tugging against the tender raw incision that opened into my belly. Then the yank would be so sudden, tears sprang from my eyes and I'd double over and drop to my knees in severe pain.

I knew our local hospital had no idea what to do concerning my feeding tube so I emailed my university physician and asked if he could remove it. Still, I had great difficulty maintaining a constant weight, fluctuating ten pounds from ninety-eight to one hundred eight pounds (my all time lowest weight was eighty-nine pounds) and if I experienced intensive episodes of vomiting or a great deal of diarrhea, it would plunge further. The weight was a dire concern and because of it, the doctor refused to remove the feeding tube. I lived in a constant state of malnourishment and dehydration. My university surgeon advised me to come in for an examination of the tube placement.

After he assessed the situation, he felt it was best to change the feeding tube to ensure it was in the correct place in my intestinal tract. The procedure was very simple and performed in his office. One purposeful tug and I let out a blood-curdling scream heard throughout the entire floor. Immediately he stopped. After my reaction, he examined the feeding tube more closely. A plastic lip on the underside of the catheter anchored the tube securely in place. Tears coursed down my checks as blood poured from the tear in my abdomen. The doctor instantly blinked away tears as well. He summoned a nurse to finish the task, refusing to inflict any more pain on me. She deadened the site, which stemmed the massive flow of blood courtesy of the blood thinners that treated the blood clot. The tender spot throbbed as though the doctor had performed surgery rather than a simple change. Two stitches held the feeding tube securely in place.

Late summer was slowly fading into fall as September days waned. Kidney stones began forcing their way through my urinary tract once again. Comfort was impossible, pain medication did nothing to soothe the ache. There was no relief, even chemically. Our only alternative was the local hospital where it would be determined if a stone was lodged requiring surgical removal and more potent pain medication could ease the torment of the piercing burred stones tearing their way through my urinary tract. We had become grossly accustomed to this process.

The local hospital agreed with my regular urologist who suggested admission to the large hospital to the north would be best so further testing could continue. The attending emergency room doctor informed us of the decision. In order to save money, we asked if my husband could possibly drive me the forty-five miles to our destination, as he'd done countless times before. However, this time the doctor had a hook for us. My husband could certainly transport me but in doing so I couldn't be given any pain medication for the trip. The only way the emergency room physician would administer medication sufficient to ease the pain was if we consented to transportation via the ambulance.

There was nothing that could be done other than concede to their wishes. I was in unbearable pain. The hospital left us little choice; intimidation was a bitter pill to swallow. We tried to be responsible and avoid an ambulance bill we knew we could not pay. From experience, we knew the expense would exceed three thousand dollars. We felt as if the hospital was using my tortuous situation against us. Of course, we realize now they had my best interest at heart. It was a very difficult time for us. The emergency room doctor gave us the options in a very threatening manner.

I repeatedly passed stones over the next eight weeks. By October 2004, my urologist had decided to perform lithotripsy to crush the nearly thirty stones located in my right kidney. The doctor warned us that lithotripsy would not be possible again for another six months, so if I continued to have large stones during this time, surgery would be the only recourse left. My kidneys had suffered considerable bruising and further damage could result in the organs sustaining significant damage beyond their ability to recover. The last thing I needed at this point was kidney failure. For three years, my health hadn't allowed me more than thirty days to pass without my admission into one of the three hospitals that became alternative homes to us.

November passed as I tried to recover from the last kidney stone bout. The holiday season was quickly approaching but I was unable to travel again this year so my family came to us. My husband stepped in and cooked for the large gathering in our home. He performed like a pro with me giving directions from the couch. He refused to let me do too much, which was extremely hard for me so I picked a centralized location and supervised.

After dinner, my sister and I decided to take our two young nephews to a movie. I hadn't left home in more than three weeks and was more than ready to venture out into the world. All during the movie, pain sliced through my abdomen at steadily increasing intensity. I shifted and squirmed in my seat but nothing seemed to ease the pain. I was soaked with sweat and shivering cold all at the same time. My mind began to panic; what was happening to me now? The pain was getting worse. I had no idea what the movie was about, the searing pain completely clouded my mind. Not knowing what to do, I endured the movie, fighting back tears of agony.

By the time we reached home, I was contemplating going to the hospital but further thought became necessary. As I took one-step outside the car, my feeding tube fell from beneath my shirt to the ground at my feet. Hurriedly my husband and sister rushed me to the hospital emergency room. We knew that time was of the essence. The opening in my abdomen would close very quickly, making reinsertion of the tube impossible without a new surgical incision.

The emergency room personnel took me right in but it was obvious they had no idea what to do. The attending physician attempted to shove a tube into the incision but could not thread the tube into the correct position. After three hours with no pain medication to help with the throbbing ache in my belly, the emergency room staff gave up and sent me home. The verdict was to contact my gastro-intestinal surgeon on Monday. He would decide what to do next.

Dread hung heavy in the aura of our home through the holiday weekend. We knew another surgical procedure was on the horizon. No matter how many times one has surgery, every instance is traumatic.

An acute yeast infection orally and vaginally resulted from the antibiotics I had been given. The doctor postponed further medical testing until mid-December when I was stronger. I was excessively weak and much depleted without the nutritional supplements. The elixir normally given via the feeding tube had yet to be replaced. Energy was non-existent because I retained so few calories each day. The scale began to take a downward turn. Malnutrition was exacting a heavy toll on my already withered body.

A dye follow-through test was to trace my digestive system. The radiology department of the large university hospital was cold and dark as the staff began to prepare me for testing. In order to deliver the dye, an intravenous line was necessary. Unfortunately, every time a vein was found, it would either collapse or burst. A phlebotomist came in from the neonatal unit who was accustomed to dealing with the smallest veins of the tiniest infants but her luck was no better than the others.

Repeatedly punctured, I tried valiantly to remain calm. I felt as if I could hardly catch my breath so mentally I chanted, "Breathe, breathe." The only other available avenue was the use of the port implanted in my chest but using it would be a last resort. The radiologist said using the port for the thick dye might render the port useless. If so, I would have to undergo surgery again to have it replaced. At this point, my condition wasn't stable enough to live without the fluids given through the port. Without the twice a week fluid infusions, I would quickly dehydrate and might not recover.

There was no other choice than to send me home without the test completed. Due to a business commitment, my husband was unable to be with me on this particular hospital visit. Our oldest son and his girlfriend stepped in to care for me and drive me to the hospital. An appointment was set to return for the dye test and to implant a new feeding tube in mid-January.

Feeling poorly, I lay down in the back seat hoping to sleep through the two and a half-hour trip home. As we drew closer to home so did the crescendo of pain. I was groaning in agony. My son did the only thing he knew to do for me. He called his dad.

"Take Mom to the emergency room," my husband told him. He'd meet us there.

"But Dad," my son said, "Mom is crying."

His dad told him we'd pay a ticket if he received one. No other response was necessary.

The diagnosis was dehydration and malnutrition. For four days, they pumped me full of fluids and nutrients. I now weighed ninety-six pounds. The last time I was this small, I was nine. I prayed to be home for Christmas. Weak, yet feeling somewhat better, I was home from the hospital on December 21st, four days before Christmas.

We made it through the holiday but I was so ill, Christmas wasn't the joyous season it should be. We made the family rounds again, which included being in the car more than eight hours, thankfully not all in the same stretch. I did little more than lay in the backseat of the car, recline on the couch and sleep under the influence of pain medication. I could barely eat and was surviving on grits, chicken and stars soup, and watered down grape juice.

All I wanted for Christmas was one good meal and my husband did his best to make sure I had it. He made thickened turkey soup served over a tiny scoop of mashed potatoes and sweet potatoes swimming in butter, my favorite corn bread dressing and the traditional jellied cranberry sauce. I could only manage two or three tablespoons at a time but after six hours I managed to clean my plate. I just knew I'd be able to handle some small smidgen of the wonderful homemade desserts and had set my sights on the thinnest sliver of chocolate pecan pie. The tiniest nibble was that one bite too many. The sugary pie set off all the bells and whistles warning me that my blood sugar disapproved vigorously. I was miserable but Christmas dinner had been very good. My compliments went to my wonderful husband, the chef. Of course, the only reward he got that day was a half smile on my face as I threw up in my ever-present bucket and dumped the entire meal. I was nauseous, cramping and in pain, but for the first time in a long time I didn't care. I had eaten Christmas dinner.

The next day, we returned to the emergency room when I couldn't keep anything down including medication. Our family doctor felt I was so malnourished, dehydrated and depleted that soon my body would be unable to sustain life. He insisted I have constant nursing care or return to the hospital. With constant care from visiting nurses and my husband, I managed to stay home through New Years' Eve. Confined to bed or the couch, with a rolling IV stand to go between the two, I remained alive and at home to welcome 2005.

January 12th rolled around and we made the trip south to the university hospital. In a wheelchair with a nurse escort, we went downstairs to the radiology department where I would get the new feeding tube. Because my blood pressure was dangerously low, the anesthesiologist could only employ twilight sleep. The drugs take you to a place where you feel as if you're floating and you never realize what the physicians are doing. Local anesthetics injected at the incision site deaden the surgical area. There I was lying on a very uncomfortable cold flat table with layers of warmed blankets to ward off the shivering cold of the operating room, loopy and really in a good mood, considering the surgeon was about to slice into my belly and thread a tube into my intestine. The incision was made and a small camera preceded the other instruments to light the way. A picture of my intestinal tract came to life on the monitor hanging above the operating table. It seemed very surreal as I watched what the doctor was doing on the screen.

For two hours, several radiologists tried to thread the tiny tube into place but each in turn failed in the attempt. My blood pressure wavered then slipped slowly into the danger zone. The procedure couldn't continue as my system could not handle any more of the relaxation medication. The radiologist shuffled into the waiting room with his head hung low. He had to admit defeat to my husband and let him know I was going into the intensive care unit. He offered no excuses, just a simple statement. "I just don't understand why this procedure is so difficult for her." The head of the radiology was away at a conference, returning the next week. A second attempt at placing the feeding tube would happen once he returned.

I remained until the second procedure on January 26th. The staff prepared me for surgery. The head of the department had returned and ready to tackle the challenge. The relaxation medication administered then my vital signs were checked. My blood pressure was low—nothing new there—but the doctors needed to know why. Several X-rays and a CAT scan later, the news was not good.

I was bleeding internally. Apparently, the bleeding originated from the right kidney, not a gross amount of blood but enough to delay the surgery again. Back to my old address, the intensive care unit for a blood transfusion. Preliminarily, the doctor assumed my kidney could no longer tolerate the large dose of blood thinners. Ordered to stop the medication a week prior to surgery, the blood thinners should be completely out of my system. After the transfusion, I got an additional pint of blood and a shot of coagulant.

A cystoscope, a test allowing the doctor to look at the interior of the bladder and the urethra, was the next order of business. It's a thin, lighted viewing instrument that, when inserted into the urethra and advanced into the bladder, will reveal any obvious defects. The doctor mended a significant tear found in my right ureter. I received an additional unit of blood to help restore my system. However, my blood was still too thin to undergo the feeding tube procedure. I would have to wait another week.

My university physician decided it would be best for me to remain in the hospital to make sure no infection developed in the kidney and to build up my system with vitamins, nutrients and fluids. Same song, different day. No amount of tears would sway the doctor's decision. The next attempt would be the last day of January. We prayed that the third time was the charm.

When the fateful day arrived, I had almost the entire hospital staff in the room or so it seemed. My university surgeon, the head radiologist, nurses and at least a dozen interns, looked on. This time the procedure worked and the feeding tube went into place, using the magnification of the CAT scan machine. Five days later, after proving I could take at least a half can (four ounces or half a cup) of the supplement in one feeding, with no passing of blood and gaining five pounds, I felt elated to be going home!

I began the long, arduous recovery process and my health seemed to be improving. For six glorious weeks, I did not step one foot inside a hospital or doctor's office. My luck didn't hold out for long. As the third anniversary of my original surgery approached on March 13, 2005, my body rejected the feeding tube once again. We had given up on our local hospital for this particular problem and put in an immediate call to my university surgeon. Because the trip south to the university hospital is a little over two hours drive, we knew that even a fast trip down there would be too late for the incision to remain open.

This time I got an upgrade in the hospital, an isolation room with a view. I could watch the sunrise over the surrounding hospital buildings. My privacy came with a price. I was kept alone, utterly alone. I could have only twenty-minute visits by no more than two people during each twelve-hour shift. Loneliness was my chief emotion during this time, the only constant in my life was the two nurses assigned to me. They catered only to me but clearly not paid to keep me company. I cried continually, depression seeped in unnoticed until I was so far in I could not find my way out. I recognized the symptoms and knew that, if allowed, this mental state would encourage the deterioration of my health. However, try as I might, I could not bring myself out of this funk.

Six days into my imposed exile, I lay in my bed sobbing when my university surgeon walked through the door with his constant posse of anxious interns. I tried to hide my tears. My red splotchy face with tear-stained cheeks was impossible to disguise. The doctor turned to his entourage, shooing them out of my room. Then this kind man sat down on the edge of my bed and said, "Okay, toots, you need to unload some of this. Let's talk."

I sat in that hospital bed, hugging my knees and blubbering. Afraid, alone, in pain, depressed and on and on. Boy, did I unload. He patted my knee and held my hand as I cried. When I finally started the sniffing and runny nose phase that always comes with constant weeping, he handed me a tissue. My ultra-professional university surgeon made one final speech, which went something like this. "You have a right to all of these feelings, every one of them. There is nothing mentally wrong with you. Anyone who didn't react this way would be unbalanced. I'm going to give you something to help manage this and you're going to take it and feel better. You can talk to your husband, a counselor, to me, your pastor or whoever will make you feel better but know this is going to be fine. We're doing everything at our disposal to make sure of it." Then he patted my knee and walked out of my room to allow me to gather myself.

When the doctor came back in with a syringe, he could obviously see the fear in my eyes. He explained to me he was starting me on something to calm my nerves for a few days, assuring me it wouldn't result in my losing control of my actions. My lovely doctor knew me well enough that he understood without my saying so that I feared the loss of my faculties. He started me on anti-depressants and explained it would take a few days for the medication to get into my system and become effective. He promised this would help me get a handle on things.

Within twenty minutes of my doctor taking his leave, my husband was walking through the door. He held me and told me the doctor had called him. He felt my health more threatened by being alone and my husband should spend as much time with me as he could. I was touched and relieved. My spirits began to rise almost immediately …maybe it was just the valium but I don't think so.

The doctor reinserted my new feeding tube the next day.

He also let us know that after a series of intravenous antibiotics over the next three days, I could go home if there were no further complications. My university surgeon felt my best interest would be better served among my own things and surrounded by family and friends. I was a happy girl.

Before dismissal from the hospital, my husband was required to attend training at my bedside. The nurse brought in this thin red hose she called a "red robin." Training on how to shove that red hose into the gapping hole in my abdomen should the feeding tube come out again was not actually a pleasant thought for him. The hose would keep the passage open until a new feeding tube could be inserted and possibly an additional incision might be involved.

During the trip home, we discussed the possibility of his actually having to use the red robin. My husband had adjusted to giving me shots, changing my IV's, changing bandages, enemas, suppositories, giving me baths, washing my hair and even shaving my legs (when I begged). He was not certain he could actually push the red robin into my body, having no idea what he might puncture or even where the tube might end up. However, when it came down to it, whatever he had to do, my husband would suck it up and do it.

Many nurses have commented to him that he could take the state nursing boards and pass them with ease. I have full confidence in him. I have always received the most wonderful care with the skill of a trained professional from a man I am so fortunate to call my husband. I am so grateful to have him in my life. I would not be alive today were it not for my loving husband. I truly owe him my life but can only give him my heart. For him, that is enough. My husband shows me his love, every day of my life.

Chapter Sixteen

~ *TREADING WATER* ~

March of 2005 marked three years since my gastric by-pass. Time for me had crept forward virtually unnoticed. I have very few memories of the days, weeks, months and years of 2002 and 2003 following the surgery. The drug-induced haze, essential in making my life at least tolerable, clouded my mind's eye. Snatches of brief recollections flicker into my consciousness from time to time but little else remains. The memories, moments and occasions of my life are irretrievable, nothing can replace the time elapsed. No one can "cure" a shattered life.

During the better part of spring, my health seemed to be somewhat stable. We always tried to enjoy these fleeting instances to the fullest while waiting for the other foot to fall. Like treading water, over time, the body will weaken and tire, then you drown.

By May, I began having tremendous trouble with my teeth. A toothache in itself is hard to endure, now it seemed when I bit into anything solid, a tooth would chip or break. My front teeth had broken in half; I was so self-conscious that when I spoke I covered my mouth. All of my teeth were loose in their sockets as if at anytime they could simply fall out. That is exactly what happened, I was talking to my best friend on the phone and felt something hard in my mouth. To avoid gagging on it, I spit it out and there in my hand was one of my teeth. I had no choice. I had to make a dental appointment.

A local dentist, who was very sensitive to patients who

were deathly afraid, was recommended. Due to an extremely bad experience during removal of my wisdom teeth, I hadn't been to a dentist in eight years. Just the thought of going in for any dental procedure, led to heart palpitations, hyperventilation and an all out panic attack. Even making the call caused my heart to race and palms to sweat. Gathering my courage, I made an appointment for a consultation. I was extremely impressed with the dentist as well as his staff. They made me feel at ease right away.

After an examination and extensive X-rays, the dentist told me that at best with considerable work, I could keep my top teeth for another year. That estimation was very conservative considering the rate my bones were eroding. He showed us on the X-rays where the roots of my teeth were scarcely hanging on in their sockets. My bottom teeth would last a little longer but in his opinion, my best option was to have the remaining upper teeth pulled and replaced with a denture. The diagnosis came as no shock to me. I had anticipated this opinion. Unfortunately, this dentist could not do the extractions, due to the possible complications. The removal of my teeth required an oral surgeon. The dentist compiled a treatment plan for me, complete with pricing, as well as detailing how he could handle my stress with medication. The dentist recommended an oral surgeon and the staff called for an appointment.

The oral surgeon concurred with the plan to do the extractions. Again, I was not surprised. Twelve teeth needed removed. The six back teeth on the first visit and after an initial healing period, the remaining six front teeth pulled six weeks later. For both sessions, the surgeon would use complete sedation. After the removal of the front teeth, the denture would be put in place—when I woke up there would be teeth in my mouth. He explained the process, then delivered a devastating blow that took me by complete surprise.

After the insurance paid their allowance, the balance would be just over three thousand dollars. The entire balance would have to be paid before the surgery. It might as well have been three million dollars because there was absolutely no way we could manage to raise that much money. With tears welling in my eyes, I bolted for the door and stood by our truck as sobs tore through my entire body. I left my husband alone inside to take care of the bill. We began the silent trip home as I sat staring out the window blinded by grief. I cried on and on knowing I would have to live with the pain, embarrassment and ugliness of my teeth. I would never be able to smile again. How could I possibly speak before people to publicize my books when it looked as though I'd been punched in the mouth leaving broken and jagged teeth? I felt like the lowest person alive and no matter how nice I appeared, my teeth would always ruin the image.

I was having an all out pity-party, feeling very sorry for myself. No matter how hard he tried, my husband could not console me. I was beyond devastated. It had taken me over a year to face the dentist, yet I finally built up enough courage to do it. I was stuck with my teeth slowly chipping away bit by bit and falling out one by one. It was grotesque to my sense of vanity.

Grief consumed me. I sobbed continually unable to bear the image staring back at me from the mirror. My sister called to find out about my appointment … all I could do was sob into the phone. Without telling me, she took matters into her own hands. She went to our dad on my behalf and convinced him to send me the money to have the dental work done. Dad called, speaking with my husband, offering to send two thousand dollars toward the dentist bill. My husband thanked him, however, we'd never be able to raise the additional thousand dollars. I had no idea any of this was taking place.

Later Dad called again and offered to cover the entire cost of the dental work. After my husband let me in on the secret, elation filled my heart. I repeatedly thanked my daddy. It was difficult to voice just how grateful I felt. Eventually I discovered my sister had coerced our dad into sending me the money. Based on that information, I didn't feel right about taking the money. I ended up calling my dad to decline his generous offer. I couldn't stand the thought of his giving me the money, knowing I couldn't afford to pay it back. I didn't want Daddy to give me the money simply because my sister made him feel guilty. In the end, Dad came through, saying he really wanted me to have my teeth fixed and his only concern was for me. He was facing retirement in a few months and would have to depend on a fixed income but he came through for me as he has my entire life. My heart swelled with love and appreciation for my daddy.

With some trepidation, I made the first appointment for surgery. The blood-thinning medication had to be discontinued until after surgery. My family doctor recommended I restrict much of my physical activity and stay off my feet as much as possible, due to the risk of the ever-present blood clot.

The time passed quickly and soon I was sitting in the dental chair prepped for surgery. An IV needle threaded into a vein in my arm and then a mask with a sickly sweet smelling scent was placed over my nose and mouth. The anesthesiologist said to breathe deeply and count down from ten. I responded, ten, nine…

The next thing I knew, I had a mouth full of gauze and was being wheeled to our truck for the ride home, given pain medication with instructions to remain off my blood-thinning medication for the remainder of the week. I was amazed there were very few problems with the back six teeth removal. This surgery was one of the easiest procedures I had ever experienced. The oral surgeon had me completely convinced of his skill and care. The fear of dentists didn't seem so bad. I wasn't so afraid at going in to have the front teeth removed.

My diet had to revert to consuming only soups and very soft foods for about a week after the surgery then I could resume my regular diet. Of course, my regular diet wasn't much different. Supplemental feedings through the feeding tube ensured that I didn't drop too much weight during the process.

Six weeks later, my regular dentist fitted me for the denture. Some sort of gooey gel squirted on a plastic plate that I was to bite down on. It left an awful feeling in my mouth, then the dental assistant, who was wonderful, had his impression to make my denture. One week later, I was to pick up the denture then return to the oral surgeon for the remaining six extractions.

The same oral surgery procedure was repeated. This time

when I awoke, I had a strange piece of plastic in my mouth. The denture was to remain in for two days then removed for cleaning. The doctor instructed me to rinse my mouth continually throughout the day with salt water to help heal the bloody sockets.

The entire process was gross. My mouth ached and I could taste the blood running down my throat. I began to be very ill, throwing up hurt even more and the bottom of the basin filled with blood. I was terrified to remove the denture but finally I did. What the plastic denture was hiding was the nastiest thing I had ever seen. Huge liver-colored blood clots clung to the roof of my mouth. I gagged uncontrollably. Swishing with salted water as instructed did little. When I spit, more blood streamed from the gapping ugly holes in my upper gums.

The largest of the awful clots clung tight. Finally, I moved it with my finger but it still clung there. Oh my God, the pain was indescribable. It felt as if I was trying to pull the gum from my mouth. Tears sprang to my eyes. I swished with the salt water again, the enormous clot finally loosened enough that I could remove it but my gums bled even more. Too large to go down the drain, I had to pick up the blood clot with tissue and flush it down the toilet.

I began to throw up in earnest. The blood, the clot…all of it made me severely nauseous. I rinsed and rinsed again, finally replacing the plastic denture in my mouth. This was awful. How could I possibly get through it? Would it ever be better?

I could hardly eat anything at all. This foreign plate in my mouth felt like it extended so far back in my mouth that I would gag and throw up often. I cried. I felt the cure was worse than the problem. I began to think my ugly, chipped teeth were not so bad after all but it was too late for that now. I consoled myself by trying to remember the situation would be short-lived.

I called our family doctor for a refill on some of my medication and while I was on the phone I mentioned to the receptionist to remind the doctor I had just had my upper teeth removed. The receptionist told me all about having the same thing done when she was much younger than I was. She assured me I'd be so happy to have had gotten dentures. Her words of encouragement, advice and concern made me feel so much better. I appreciated her sensitivity more than she will ever know. There was an end in sight and eventually the situation would improve. I looked forward to that part.

There were places on my gums which were so sore from the plastic rubbing against them, I could hardly stand it. I was in intense pain. I called my regular dentist and scheduled an appointment for realignment (almost sounds like having your tires done). The jovial dental assistant worked with me constantly to make sure the denture fit. I was assured I shouldn't have any painful areas. He squirted a jelly substance on my denture and replaced it in my mouth. This would form a cushion between my sensitive, aching gums and the plastic denture. We did several fittings and finally were both satisfied with the way my new teeth fit. Swelling was definitely an issue and the denture would require refitting several times to accommodate for that.

A very difficult period followed. I had to learn how to eat with artificial teeth. Coping with a large plastic piece in my mouth was very awkward. I gagged constantly. At first I thought it was just my being unaccustomed to the denture. When I returned to the dentist to have a fitting, the denture tech took one look and told me the denture was simply too large for my mouth. Dentures continue, to this day, to be an uphill battle that I am still trying to cope with.

The denture left a terrible taste in my mouth. Bits of food often found their way beneath it causing sudden excruciating pain to the roof of my mouth. When I sneeze or throw up (as I often do), I (still to this day) have to physically hold my teeth in or they will come flying out like a plastic torpedo. Just to contend with something foreign in my mouth was uncomfortable. Even to me this sounds like whining. Many millions of people have dealt with dentures, having the same sort of difficulty. For me, it was just one more burden with which to deal.

The dental adjustment was just plain difficult. When you deal with a multitude of problems, one more thing seems to be like "the straw that broke the camel's back." Speaking, eating, brushing my teeth, and caring for my swollen and sore gums were all arduous undertakings. The thought of even kissing my husband again scared me to death. I carefully cleaned my mouth every two hours. Eventually, or so I have been told, I'd get used to the false teeth and it will be as though the denture is not even there. I haven't quite gotten there yet, today, several years later.

Eating with the denture has been quite a learning experience. Companies show how easy it is to eat corn on the cob, an apple or steak with no problems at all. I haven't quite figured out how to eat those things and many others as yet. Speaking without the denture clicking or making that whistling sound against my palate has been a challenge.

Anytime I have to take out the denture, I hide behind the locked bathroom door. I don't want anyone to see me without teeth. The sight is quite disgusting to me. I understand this opinion is vanity run amuck, but I have only looked at myself in the mirror a few times without my denture. When one is self-conscious, even in front of your own image, it can be debilitating. Ten pounds dropped from my frame during this period; the loss was ten pounds I didn't have to lose.

However, there is an upside. Recently, I had a photo shoot for one of my books and I smiled, showing my new teeth in a picture for the very first time in my life. I was amazed at how well the photographs turned out. My teeth looked wonderful, straight and pearly white. I am very proud of that picture. It has been an ordeal getting here and one I never want to repeat.

As I tried to deal with my new teeth, the feeding tube began to give me problems again. It would draw in so tightly against my tender stomach that I could hardly stand the pain. Unlike the previous situation, the tube was not popping back out again. The incision where the tube entered my body began to bleed and leak gastric fluid or bile. I had never experienced this before except for my original surgery when the incision was infected.

I panicked, sending a hasty email to my university doctor asking if perhaps he would please remove the feeding tube. He asked about my weight, throwing up, diarrhea, etc. My weight hovered around one hundred fifteen pounds and seemed to have stabilized since the drop after my dental work. The weight gain was largely due to a diet based on a lot of over-cooked pasta. My husband would cook pasta to nearly a mush stage then mix it with minced chicken and Alfredo sauce. This meal had become a daily staple for me. Everyone else in the family was sick at the sight of it again!

I continued to vomit frequently and diarrhea was common for me. The doctor emailed me and suggested that perhaps some of the fluid should be removed from the balloon anchoring the feeding tube in my intestine in an effort to relieve the blockage the balloon was most likely creating. To confirm the diagnosis an X-ray was necessary then if needed the fluid could be removed from the balloon in the doctor's office. With my weight dropping below the one hundred twenty mark, I was underweight. He didn't feel that at this point I was stable enough to have the tube removed. The doctor's decision left me feeling depressed but I understood his position. He understood my feelings but had to consider my body as a whole.

I just wanted to stay out of the hospital. I had survived for the longest stretch in more than three years without admission. Releasing some of the fluid from the anchor bulb seemed to relieve some of the pain. For now, I had avoided the hospital and prayed the doctor could make sure we maintained this path.

During June 2005, I contracted a bacterial infection causing a massive coverage of blood blisters over my entire body. It was not painful but it looked dreadful and itched. The episode lasted nearly six weeks with continuous antibiotics, baths of witch hazel and an oatmeal-based water additive. It was extremely important that none of the blisters burst due to my bleeding problems. The unsightly blotches finally faded.

The doctor diagnosed the situation. My body had gone into starvation mode and was feeding on my own connective tissues. Of course, this was probably the fifth or sixth time this situation had occurred. Because I had been unable to ingest the protein my body required to sustain life, instinctively, my body was trying to survive by feeding on itself. The bacterial infection resulted from one of the blood blisters which had burst. My immune system was so low the infection soon invaded my blood. Resolving the infection meant massive doses of antibiotics again.

The antibiotics caused problems as well. A yeast infection developed in my mouth, cracking both sides of my lips, which hurt terribly. Even worse, I couldn't stand to wear the denture. My tongue swelled and felt as if it were on fire. As a result, I couldn't eat and my weight began to decline again. The only thing sustaining me was the feeding tube. As if this situation weren't bad enough, I developed a yeast infection down below. Anything going into my mouth was excruciating and anything coming out left me in tears. I was in sad shape. My university surgeon had been right. My health was not stable. Would it ever be?

My family doctor prescribed medication to swish in my mouth and a capsule for the other end. After ten days of agony, I began to feel better. Thankfully, we endured this episode without having to go to the hospital. This was certain progress!

Chapter Seventeen

~ ONE MORE CHAPTER IN MY LIFE ~

A simple telephone call in July 2005 was the beginning of an extremely tumultuous time for me. The words "medical leave" struck terror in my heart. I phoned my university surgeon for a refill and his patient coordinator casually informed me that he had become ill and would probably be out for six weeks. The office was in the process of turning over all patients to another doctor in the same office whom I had never met.

I mentally calmed myself, concentrated on my breathing, which was coming in short gasps, but maybe this physician would be as caring and attentive as my university surgeon. Though even with the mental justifications that perhaps this was not so bad, I sobbed into my pillow. I felt as if I had no one to turn to, medically speaking, who truly understood the numerous complications I dealt with every day of my life. On the other hand, I was extremely concerned about my doctor's health. I had come to care and respect this man. He is an exceptional individual. He had so many irons in the fire, I'm certain he didn't have a private moment for himself or his family. It was my opinion he'd simply worked himself into exhaustion. I emailed him to wish him well and hoped to see him soon. It was some time before I received a response of any kind from him.

I had an appointment for a follow-up exam at the university medical center just a few weeks away; so I began to clear my thoughts to give the new doctor a chance. My health was precariously stable but I remained unable to eat solid foods, vomiting several times a day and suffering from irregular bowel problems. The ever-present yeast infection continued to plague me, erupting in my mouth then spreading to my most intimate parts. My raw and bleeding mouth often resulted in receiving my only nourishment through the feeding tube.

Once I arrived for my appointment, all of my worst fears were recognized. The doctor was a relic, left from some bygone era. He was certainly knowledgeable concerning my condition, explaining he'd spent hours reading my ridiculously cumbersome medical history. The doctor had no bedside manner, tact nor sympathy for my condition. I had promised myself I'd never tolerate a doctor who acted in a derogatory manner ever again. In his opinion, I should be walking two or three miles every day to regain some strength, forcing food and being weaned from the feeding tube. Generally his advice was, "girl, pull up your bootstraps and bulldoze your way into good health" or at least that's what I interpreted from his examination comments. He did give me a prescription to help alleviate some of the constipation that seemed to constantly plague me, other than that I was on my own. I cried in the darkness of our truck all the way home. Consciously, I realized that I couldn't fault my regular doctor for ill health, nonetheless I felt rejected and alone.

For a short time we experienced an all new blissful feeling. Normalcy. Grabbing every spare moment of stable health that came along, I devoured the opportunity to finally go to press with my latest book. "Get Off the Interstate: The True Stories Behind Florida's East Coast Historical Markers", Volume II in my "Get Off the Interstate" series. After convincing a local printer to take a chance on me and print the books with the understanding I could buy them a few at a time as I could afford them. I regret to say, the proposition didn't turn out too well for him. Because of my continued ill-health the "Florida Book", as we call it, hasn't received nearly the publicity, promotion or sales that it deserves. The lady who handled the transaction was absolutely wonderful and really put her neck on the line for me. I didn't live up to my side of the bargain. I deeply regret and apologize profusely but there was nothing I could do to change the situation.

I was nonetheless very proud of the "Florida Book". It's an incredible mass of work (if I do say so myself and I do!). I dare say there has never been a book of its comparison and the information it imparts is one of the most dramatic and all-consuming historical wonder-work on the market today. That said by its proud Mom, me! If the book ever catches on in Florida, it will be at least a state-wide best seller. This was simply another goal I had simply prayed I could finish. Of course, now I'm praying for the "South Carolina book" (it will certainly take several more years, but I've started and that's progress in the right direction) as well as this little diatribe.

The respite failed to last. Soon, we had started the constipation regime again. For two weeks nearing fall 2005, the situation grew continually worse. My husband called the new university physician, who offered no help at all, advising to keep up laxative/enema routine, have me eat more roughage and bran. Right…! Then I would be in the hospital for sure. The gas pains alone would be enough to win me a visit to the emergency room, or worse yet, hospital admissions.

My husband telephoned our family doctor. He suggested I come in. The diagnosis was impaction. Since the constipation medication wasn't working, he suggested an "evacu-kit." Simply put, this awful drink (luckily the gunk could go through my feeding tube) is used before surgery to clean out the intestinal tract. It is very powerful stuff. Two ounces later, I was sitting on the toilet screaming in pain. Off to the emergency room we go.

The nursing staff at the ER tried warm water soap enemas and strong laxatives prescribed by our family physician. The nurses worked with me for six hours to relieve the rock hard masses impacting my bloated intestinal tract. Nothing worked and because pain medication slows the intestinal process, I couldn't have any medication to help with the cramping. I began to vomit then. My system was so dehydrated and worn-out, I physically collapsed.

Unable to give me any relief, the staff phoned the doctor and I found myself tucked into a hospital bed once again. X-rays with marking dye contrast would reveal how involved in the intestinal system the blockage went. The results revealed I had four major obstructions at various points and only pin-point veins of the dye were getting through at all.

The doctor tried to manually, as in shoving a gloved hand into my already tormented rectum, to remove the clots he could reach. The alleviation of the strictured intestine never happened. He called in a local gastrointestinal doctor to try to remove the blockage and though it was obvious, he was leery about treating me with all of my medical baggage, he did cautiously examine me. Our physician advised us that if the specialist failed to clear my system rather quickly, I was facing surgery within the next twenty-four hours. A procedure that detailed could not be performed locally and with my university physician unavailable, we would be left at the hands of someone new and unknown. We prayed.

The local gastric doctor arrived several hours later but was very honest with us that because my system was so irregular, he could only offer basic medical treatment. He mixed what he called a "special cocktail" and pumped it through my feeding tube. I have never been so grateful for that feeding tube than I was at that moment. The liquid was noxious. I could smell it as it pumped through. A whiff of it was something between rotten seafood and a septic tank. Within thirty minutes, clots exploded from my butt like torpedoes fired from a tube. Much to our amazement, relief came very quickly. God heard our prayers and answered, though not in any usual form. Finally, the nurses issued pain medication and my system was flushed completely with plain warm water enemas. Like magic, the pain in my gut disappeared, though I had a very tender bottom. The saying, "this too shall pass" had new meaning.

My regular university physician returned in October 2005. I was so relieved and happy to see him. However, his appearance was a shock; he had lost considerable weight and looked very pale. We were concerned that he possibly had some life-threatening disease, cancer perhaps. There was little in the way of explanation offered other than he had severe juvenile diabetes. Soon we were down to business. After reading my family doctor's notes, he told us he'd like to do some follow-up testing. Do not pass go. Do not go home. I checked into my usual hospital suite and settled in for the duration.

The radiologist treated me to a colonoscopy the next morning. Thankfully, I was in a state of sedated oblivion. The doctor prescribed a massive influx of fluids to saturate my system. True to form as soon as the fluids flooded my system, I began to pass kidney stones. One, two, three, four… (Oh, golly is there any more? Sorry, I just couldn't resist the little rhyme). The count continued to climb every time I mounted the dreaded toilet seat. The doctor decided that maybe something should be done other than treat the symptomatic pain.

A university urologist was urgently summoned when I began passing blood from my kidneys. Then my temperature began to soar out of control with no relief in sight. I had an infection. However, I guess I was in the right place at the right time, no need to rush to the emergency room this time. More blood work followed to find an antibiotic suitable to fight the resistant infection which refused to respond when traditional antibiotics were infused. Everyone was extremely frustrated with my condition, yet no one could properly diagnose the problem, therefore appropriate medication was basically a shot in the dark.

The unfortunate phlebotomists, vampires, descended on me for the blood draw to no avail. They found that it was nearly impossible to get a vein to remain viable long enough to get a sufficient blood sample and testing required numerous vials. My veins would roll, disappear, or simply burst on contact. I suggested that possibly blood could be taken from my port, that was one of its primary purposes. Nope, could not be done, I don't know why. So I lay silently there in the hospital bed while being stabbed repeatedly in every appendage front to back. Finally, finally, a neo-natal nurse collected a sample large enough to conduct the testing.

The doctor arrived the next morning armed with test results by the ream. I had an infection, duh… and we didn't even have a medical degree. The tricky part was the bacteria happened to be an uncommon, unidentified strain. See, I do nothing the easy way. University physicians specializing in disease control were put on alert to determine what we were dealing with. They dealt directly with the Center for Disease Control in Atlanta. Once again I was a "special" girl. It would take three to ten days before any results were in. At that time, the doctors could determine the bacteria then treatment options. So I was to lay there until test results and a plan of action were in hand for my posse of doctors.

A colonoscopy brought attention to an area of my colon that had herniated due to the recent severe constipation and impaction. A second dye test was performed to see just how bad the colon leakage appeared. The results were not favorable. Two sections of bowel had actually blown out from the sheer force behind the obstructions. We faced a catch twenty-two situation. I needed surgery to repair or remove the areas of leaking colon. The small ruptures were spewing waste into my system, flowing poison throughout my body. Sharp, jagged, burr-like stones had left paper-cut like tears as they ripped through the ureter trying to make their way to the bladder leaving another infection. The tiny cuts leaked enormous amounts of blood internally, primarily due to the blood-thinners prescribed when the blood clot formed in my right thigh. The doctor ordered a unit of blood each day for five days. I wasn't comfortable receiving the blood because things happen and all of the sudden you are deathly ill from some blood-borne disease. With my luck, I'd be the unfortunate one in a million. However, a roll of the dice with disease is less likely than a stroke resulting from the blood clot. Four doses of coagulant had finally stopped the internal bleeding. The fever still raged and I was moved to intensive care.

My doctor walked into the room early the next morning and sat on the edge of my bed, looking very grim. His long face made me dread the talk we were about to have. As delicately as possible, he told me we'd be moving into the operating room within the hour. It was now imperative the blowouts in my intestine get immediate attention. The ureter had several large gashes requiring repair as well, therefore, a urology surgeon would be on stand-by to perform that highly specialized repair following the first procedure. The surgeon cautioned that in my critical situation, the procedure could be potentially dangerous, the certain alternative was much more distasteful—death.

Strangely enough, because of my repeated visits to the surgical suite at this huge university hospital, I had come to know the nurses and technicians, not only by their first names but I also knew many of their children's names! I wasn't so nervous going in, I had complete confidence in my doctors and I think they had given me some pretty good drugs to help me relax as well. The surgery lasted six very long hours for my family, the time moved slowly. They were afraid to leave, even for meals, in case the situation went south or the surgeon made an appearance.

When the nurse gently prodded me from the deep sedation, I recovered enough to realize the intense pain. The attending nurse summoned my husband, who would be the only person allowed access to me for the next forty-eight hours. My sister sat in the waiting room sobbing, the anticipation just too much. The surgeon cleaned-up and joined my family for his report. He sat down among them and gave a great sign. He clearly didn't take any pleasure in describing the outcome of this procedure. The doctor removed thirty-six inches of colon. As a result, I'd have to endure the use of a colostomy bag until my body could heal, and with any luck, which we prayed would befall us, the doctor could remove the bag. Because I continued to run a fever, I would enjoy the hospitality of the Intensive Care Unit (ICU) for a while longer.

Of course staying in the unit was anything but pleasant. I wasn't allowed to see anyone with the exception of my husband who had to wear what he called, "full body armor", due to the tremendous risk of infection. Privately, the doctor pulled my husband aside to give him further explanation of my condition. I had gone into shock during surgery. In fact, my heart had stopped. Emergency resuscitation measures saved my life. I was alive but remained in critical condition. The next forty-eight hours were precarious. The doctor explained if I lived through the next two days my chances for long-term recovery improved. I was oblivious and felt that since I had come out of the surgery everything would be just fine.

Obviously, I did survive. The doctor informed us before my release that if the impaction continued, he would remove my colon completely. It is as gross as it sounds, I would never produce a solid poop ever again. The biggest problem being, I'd have to endure almost constant IV hydration to replace the fluid loss. We prayed this fate could be avoided. Many people ask, why I say "we." Believe me, my husband suffers through all of this torture with me and feels my pain as intensely as if it were his own, though you'd never know it, except for brief moments of total exhaustion.

After six very long weeks, I was happy to see my home again. The doctor cautioned us that I required total isolation at home for another two weeks. Should I spike a temperature of more than one hundred degrees, to summon an ambulance immediately. Homeward bound. Home sweet home. I've never been so happy to see any place in my life. Home. I actually felt at times as if I would never make it back there. Recovery still proved to be very slow in coming.

Grim news faced us at home. This time it wasn't me or my health in jeopardy. My father-in-law was diagnosed with inoperable lung cancer. The prognosis was not good. His time was short, maybe a year. My husband felt torn between taking care of me and desperately snatching whatever time he had left with his dad. He went to his father's side for two days and then quickly returned to me. I put on a good front and encouraged him to return to seize every precious moment he could with Dad.

Visiting nurses checked on me daily, administering antibiotics and fluids. He felt confident enough concerning my recovery to make the trip over and spend time with Dad, along with all of his sisters, who had also gathered ranks. Little more than basic comfort and pain management was possible for Dad's condition. He refused any sort of other treatments. So they simply spent what precious time was left by his side. After a week spent to commiserate with his family, my husband returned home to tend the business and me. We were shocked when we received an urgent call only two weeks later. Dad was quickly losing the battle with cancer. He was calling for his only son, so without a moment's hesitation, he left.

I began experiencing a familiar pain, signaling that the feeding tube was about to give me problems. I kept that little informational tidbit to myself. My husband and I talked every day, it obvious that Dad wasn't going to be with us much longer. My younger son was very worried about me so he tattled to his father. My husband and I got into a very intense argument over the phone the next evening, he actually yelled at me. He was terribly upset I hadn't told him what was happening. We both knew he'd return home immediately were it necessary.

This wonderful man struggled with the decision. After many hours of conversation, I was able to convince him to stay with his father. I made a solemn vow that if my situation grew worse, I would summon him immediately. The intense guilt I felt was very hard for me to deal with. I wanted to be there beside my husband while he endured this awful time. I longed to see my father-in-law one last time. I was so upset by the situation I failed to take the last opportunity I had to speak to Dad over the phone. I regret that to this day. Logically, we knew I was unable to make the trip.

Dad lived only six weeks after his initial diagnosis. He'd lost Mom and a good many of his closest friends over the last two years. We felt he was simply ready to go, yet this knowledge did nothing to relieve the pain of his loss. We were so happy we'd made the decision for my husband to remain there to the end. A wonderful man was lost and we felt his absence very deeply. An incredible military service with the assistance of the Marine Corps, to which he was deeply devoted, was held staging a fitting tribute. Once a Marine, always a Marine. He believed strongly in my writing and supported me from day one. I still miss him to this day.

Our entire family gathered for the funeral, sharing the dark days that followed. Gratefully, my husband's "adopted" brother provided us with a hotel room where I could get away from it all and rest. He was so considerate to be so concerned for me. He will never know how much I appreciated the gesture. We remained there for just over a week. My husband tended to family matters and I remained in the hotel just to be near him. Finally, we returned home, exhausted and in no mood for the holiday season. We did some last minute shopping, trying to observe the festive occasion for our sons. It was a futile attempt.

On December 28th, 2005, my feeding tube fell out. My husband quickly put his medical training to use, slipping the red robin replacement tube into the vacated hole in my abdomen. It was easier than we thought. Because of the New Years' holiday, we couldn't get a scheduled appointment at the university hospital until January 3rd. We did our best to maintain the tube path until we could get to the doctor to have the feeding tube inserted. As 2006 dawned, little had changed in my condition. We prayed this year would be a turning point. It wasn't.

When we finally managed to get into the hospital, the original incision was infected. The doctor scheduled surgery to clean the wound, remove dead and decayed tissue. Once the doctor viewed the situation from the inside, he also removed thirty-six ounces of scar tissue. The infection made it necessary for another series of antibiotics before the surgeon replaced the tube. The surgery to remove scar tissue and drain the original wound of infection were simple procedures, since there were no other complications, I returned home three days later minus the feeding tube which was to be replaced at a later date.

After we returned home, the surgeon called us twice a week for an update on my condition. Little did we know this hospital stay would be the last time we'd see my beloved university doctor. The very first call came with devastating news. Due to his own medical concerns, my university physician was taking a much-needed medical retirement. I was stuck with the ancient doctor taking his place. The sadness was overwhelming and I sank into a dark depression over the situation.

We immediately agreed I'd have to find another gastric doctor to attend me, the mere thought of the search left me exhausted before the pursuit. It was a dreaded process finding a suitable gastrointestinal doctor/surgeon, then having them experienced enough with gastric by-pass complications to deal with my damaged body. Briefing a new doctor on all I have endured, and continue to face every day, was an ordeal we hated the thought of. My case was no small undertaking for anyone.

Also, as the fourth anniversary of my gastric by-pass approached, we knew there was one last chance to bring some sort of legal action against the original surgeon. Medical malpractice suits in Georgia may not exceed four years after the subject initial procedure. Of course, the law varies from state to state. We verified the dates, then selected a local attorney to handle the case. He came very highly recommended so we felt safe with him. I called for an appointment then we proceeded to gather every scrap of medical paperwork we could get. The massive sheath of paper "evidence," array of X-rays and test results filled the entire backseat of our car. No one could've found space to hide a paperclip, much less sit down. We planned to face the attorney loaded to the teeth. My husband had to drive this process virtually on his own, I was despondent. I felt as if every bit of reserve energy had ebbed away, every day it seemed harder and harder to go on.

Our appointed time to see the attorney came two weeks later. I was unable to climb the stairs to his office. We presented my situation to him and, in his opinion, we seemed to have a case but he would have to look into the finer points of the complaint. He planned to turn over a copy of my files to a lawyer/doctor who was supposedly an expert in gastric by-pass and medical malpractice. Then we waited and waited, then continued to wait. I called every so often to check on the case. However, when you're busy trying to survive, pursuing a lawsuit is not your primary concern.

The lawyer contacted us, in order to continue the case to gather additional information he needed—three-hundred fifty dollars. My husband scraped the money together somehow. How we could afford to eat, I'm not sure. We still expected the best possible outcome of the lawsuit. We never wanted to win millions or even a fortune of any kind; we would be happy if my medical bills could somehow get paid.

The days before March 13th, 2006, the fourth anniversary deadline for eligibility to go forward with litigation rolled by with NASCAR speed. We contacted the lawyer again. His secretary scheduled a meeting. It was there, during that meeting when he informed us that in his opinion we had no case. The only explanation we received was that "the surgery was done within acceptable medical parameters," in the opinion of the lawyer/doctor "expert" who was consulted. I felt that no one outside of those who loved me, was concerned about my well-being. Was there no end to the loss that this doctor cost us?

I felt as if the agony we had somehow lived through these past four years meant nothing, swept aside, my life was meaningless. The quality of my life, everything lost, including nearly three years of my life in which I remember little of, due to the pain, the sheer agony, mind-numbing medication, and illness so intense I've blocked even the faintest memory. My career, income, time with my family, friends, financial stability, my teeth, my health, life as we knew it. The list can go on and on but wrap it all up and still all of this counted for NOTHING. My life was not worth this doctor's reputation. This expert witness/lawyer blatantly declared my life was virtually worthless and my family would have been better off financially if I had died. I felt like the lowest form of life. I felt pain born of emotion. My husband harbors (to this day) incredible bitterness toward the doctor, hospital, the attorneys and the legal system. When anyone inquires about my health, the typical response is "you should sue" then the irate tirade of anger comes spewing forth from my wonderful husband who is more than entitled to his feelings.

Further, what do I feel about all this? Guilt, an overwhelming sense of guilt permeates my entire being. My decision to have this surgery, this elective surgery, has put my family into crisis. My decision to have this surgery has put constant strain on my family and friends worrying over me. My decision to have this surgery has cost my husband clients because he has spent the majority of his time taking care of me. My responsibility for hurting others, who I love, because I wanted to be thin is enormous …financially, we will never recover. If this sounds like a rant, I'm sorry. It's taken me a long time to say I'm angry and I'm entitled to my anger. I'll say it again. I am entitled to be angry. All that's left for me is anger. Unfortunately, like my frequent infections, this pent-up rage grows and festers if it goes unchecked. It's taken a long time to place the blame where it is due, but at the heart of my problems is the doctor who performed my original surgery and he isn't worthy of the energy spent to hate him.

We hardly had time to catch our breath as spring 2006 approached. I was weak and not growing much better as the days passed. Soon we found ourselves tucked away in the university hospital again, awaiting a new report from the Center for Disease Control in Atlanta to explain a recurrent fever and continued down-hill turn of my health. We were simply left with, "What now?"

Chapter Eighteen

~ WHAT NOW? ~

I had my usual nurse, usual room in ICU as a blazing fever left the Atlanta CDC befuddled. They poured over my blood work, tasked with the identification of a bacterial strain or source of infection that threatened my very existence, again. After nine days I was moved to an isolation room, which was totally sterile. It meant that unlike ICU, I could see other family members and friends. Not many people had the opportunity to travel the extended distance to the university hospital two hours from our home and nearly six hours from the remainder of my family. I did get a chuckle with everyone who did come through the door. Hospital policy, because of my now non-existent immune system, required all visitors to wear bright yellow anti-bacterial suits for my protection against outside germs. I referred to my visitors as "banana people." At least I had something to lighten my dark mood.

The CDC reported that somehow I had contracted a common yeast infection, however, I had managed to have it show up in my blood. There was no explanation for this condition, it was rare to have a blood yeast infection but somehow I managed to find a way! Again, I'm a "special" girl and could almost do the medically impossible. More high-powered antibiotics followed. The antibiotic used to kill the infection was so potent that it destroyed all of my body's defenses. I was left vulnerable to every sniffle. A common cold could do me in for good. So to counteract any bacteria near me, I had to take a second series of medication to protect me against the first. The fever abated after four days, but I had no energy, though it didn't really matter at this point—I couldn't leave the isolation room. A trip to the bathroom was as far as I traveled and such a scenic stroll it was, all four feet of it.

I worked on my current book project during my long hours alone in the hospital. I'm committed to at least two hours a day functioning as a writer (author?), when I'm able to manage it, (I like to think of myself as a professional author anyway, of course, if you read something I've written that's totally off the wall, now you understand why). But that two hours leaves twenty-two others, some of which are dedicated to, let's make a list: pain, medical tests, medical procedures, vital signs at least two-hundred times a day, including midnight, four-o'clock and six-o'clock in the morning then there is sleep and medicated oblivion. Otherwise my days were very lonely. My husband had to bring in an income just to keep our utilities on and gas in the vehicles, not to mention the silly little habit of our eating rather regularly. Not so much me, but the remainder of my family liked dinner on a regular basis. Other than that, we paid very few of our bills. I'm not proud of it but that's just how it was.

Due to the infection in my mouth, it felt burned inside. The pain was excruciating. I could not tolerate any sort of "real" food. I was living on Jell-O, pudding, ice cream and room temperature weak chicken broth. Everything had to be sugar-free and nothing really had any taste. I was just eating out of habit three times a day and finally gave up on that, too. Putting anything in my mouth was not worth the pain and effort. The doctor finally decided we had no choice but to replace the feeding tube. By this time I was indifferent, I was getting worn out with this constant struggle to survive. In addition to the infection in my mouth, my most private parts burned, itched and bled now. I don't know which hurt worse, the top or bottom. I put off going to the bathroom until I felt as if my bladder might explode. The pain was unbearable, the itch was relentless, my frustration built every day. The doctor had ordered a cream that didn't help, then out of desperation, the doctor ordered a topical numbing gel that would relieve the pain, but even that only worked for a very short time. Because of possible tissue damage, even the gel could only be used very short-term.

Early one morning, a doctor walked into my room as I lay curled in a tight ball, sobbing. He was not a constant in my life and for the life of me, I can't even remember his name. I got the impression he was simply the doctor assigned to my case on this particular day. That's just how it is in these huge medical teaching facilities when you have no "personal physician." His demeanor was caring and kind when he sat down on the edge of my bed and took my hand. He asked what was going on. I could barely speak as the emotional turmoil tore from my throat in great gulps. At this point, I had endured so much I was involved in a total emotional meltdown, overwhelmed and depressed. We sat there side by side for about twenty minutes. He turned his face away from me as I tried to compose myself. When I finally controlled my breathing, this physician was very sympathetic to my plight and simply listened as I poured out my heart.

Pain, loneliness, vomiting, diarrhea, despair over my continued complications had gotten the better of me. The constant nagging ache of my body rarely let up unless I received enough medication to bring on a sedated sleep. Violent spasms convulsed my body after taking even the smallest sip of water, when my system was emptied, bitter tasting yellow bile spewed forth from what seemed like the pit of hell. Diarrhea left me limp, sapping the last of my waning energy. Lifting my head seemed like a chore, the thought of doing anything even as mundane as eating dinner felt like hard manual labor. Because we had to have some sort of income, it was necessary for my husband to remain at home for at least several days a week; therefore I lay alone two hours away from home with no one to talk to, no one who loved me to help soothe my torturous days or even a shoulder to cry on. Friends and family burned up the telephone lines but still loneliness was a constant companion. Mentally, I understood. Emotionally, I was feeling sorry for myself and shut off from everyone I knew and loved.

The doctor listened intently while I vented, then thoughtfully he said, "I understand." He calmly let me know I was completely justified in all of my feelings. His decision was that I could receive treatment at home which would make me feel better mentally if not physically, if I promised to obey all of the contact restrictions. He ordered home healthcare nurses to come in twice a day to administer fluids, intravenous antibiotics and nutritional supplements. My spirits brightened and I called my husband immediately to take me home. He made the trip to get me that evening and by the time he arrived, I was sitting on the edge of the bed, fully dressed with every last thing packed and ready to head out the door. By eight o'clock, I was securely ensconced on the couch in our living room, a much happier girl. I never saw that particular physician again.

Again, I was sentenced to two weeks under house arrest, unable to leave the confines of my home due to the dangers of contracting some new source of infection. My autoimmune system remained extinct at this point, very much like an aids patient. Thankfully, that was a battle I hadn't been subjected to, though it was always a possibility. God Bless those who have to endure that terrible disease. I don't know that pain but I can sympathize. The nurses visited twice daily and took wonderful care of me. After exactly fifteen days, I spiked a high fever again. I just couldn't win.

Returning from the mailbox, my husband looked in on me as I apparently lay napping on the couch in our living room. When he drew closer, he realized my eyes were open but vacant and seemingly unseeing. I failed to respond when he gently touched my face. I had a deathly pallor, my skin both clammy and blazing hot. Somewhere far, far away, I could hear his voice calling my name and felt the rousing but forceful pats on my cheeks. Though I tried to form words, my mouth moved but no sound came forth. I felt my senses fade into blackness. I remembered nothing else for days.

Never one to panic, or even to let emotions guide his path, my husband quickly formed a plan of action. He called one of the nurses assigned to care for me who happened to live just a few doors down from our home. Luckily, she was home and rushed to my side. After taking my vitals, she noted that my temperature soared over one hundred four and my body had slipped into shock. She immediately took over the situation and called the county 911 rescue. Soon the blaring of sirens and flashing lights brought excitement to our usually quiet neighborhood. First the red fire engine arrived, followed closely by the ambulance and the sheriff's department. Everybody in the county has to come out when there is an emergency and I think they report it in the local newspaper as well. The emergency personnel assessed my situation, loaded me into the ambulance and within a span of fifteen minutes, I was on my way to the local hospital emergency room.

The triage doctor looked at me briefly and could make no determination what had suddenly happened to plunge me into distress. Our family doctor was called and his office manager informed us that unless we could pay our outstanding debt, he would be unable to advise us further. Very professional, very callous (of course, the doctor had no idea I was in severe distress), an office manager with no concern for patient care only takes care of billing. We were left on our own to fend for ourselves. What now indeed? We didn't have time to worry with this at the moment, I was beyond caring and my husband was simply scared this would be our final moments together.

It was the consensus of the emergency room staff, the MRSA had returned. My stats didn't paint a pretty picture: temperature dangerously high, blood pressure low and dropping, blood oxygen levels not good, breathing low and shallow, heart rate soaring. Even through the various reviving techniques, I failed to respond and reluctantly the doctor reported to my husband that once they managed to stabilize my condition enough for transport, life flight was to be called and I'd be moved to a larger, better equipped hospital nearby. Quickly, my husband vetoed this idea and called the university medical center that had cared for me in the past.

I was intubated and hooked to every sort of monitor available, intravenous lines pumped in fluids to try and keep me alive—stable was simply too much to ask. The doctor determined I was in a comatose state, probably due to the fever. Life flight arrived and I was whisked away. My husband along with our baby boy drove the just over one hundred miles to the hospital. My guys refused to let any thoughts of my demise creep into their minds. Just another crisis, just another obstacle, and just another hill we had to climb before eventually we'd see the other side of this situation, too. Three days in a coma, fourteen days in intensive care, eleven more in isolation and sixteen in a regular hospital room. The tally added up slowly but indeed, we did come out on the other side once again.

I had always been taught that God will never give you more than you can bear but I began to doubt that sentiment. He obviously has a plan for me, I truly believe that, though I'd really like to know what he has in mind. Maybe it is this book. Maybe it's to show me just how strong I can be, maybe bringing me closer to those I love or closer to him, I sincerely don't know but all those things have occurred. He did bring me to my wonderful church family that have become so very close to me now and I suppose even something as simple as bringing organized religion back into my life might be his only reason for putting me through all this. Believe me, I love God but don't think (at least I hope) he didn't go to all these lengths just to get me back into church. I'd have gone with much less encouragement.

The beginning of the year had passed in an ill-fated blur but a brighter side was on the horizon … sort of. By the summer of 2006, we finally had a respite from the ugliness that had engulfed me earlier in the year. My health seemed better. I was nearly (dare I say it!) healthy for the first time in a very long time. This was indeed a new experience. We went about living our lives almost routinely, the relief was intoxicating. I began seeing another family doctor and she tended to my "everyday" needs (constipation, diarrhea, vitamins, swelling, headaches, backaches, sinus problems, etc., etc.). I had no regular gastric doctor besides the ancient relic at the university and I wouldn't be seeing him again. Then there was my ever present local urologist who has hung in there for the duration, bless his heart. The only bad thing about my new family doctor was as usual she had a nasty, cold-hearted office manager … I think that must be in the job description. Every time I went in, she hounded me for money. It got to the point that I just suffered the minor stuff (like yeast infections and low grade fevers) in silence without a doctors care because she was so awful to me. Really, I do understand that it was her job, but the doctor knew my situation when she took me on and my medical insurance was paying her a small fortune. Why wasn't that enough? Insurance and medical billing professionals, I'll never understand either.

The mail was another thing altogether. We had a cardboard box and trash can situated by the front door. Junk mail in file Thirteen and all medical, credit card, non-essential bills in file Thirteen-A (that's what we called the box). We didn't even open the bills in Thirteen-A anymore, there was no point. We often had to decide which was more important—electricity or phone, water or food, gas or car insurance. The mortgage was three months behind. We knew that more than those few months, they would begin foreclosure proceedings. Our family and friends had done everything humanly possible to help keep us afloat financially but there is only so much other people can do before they end up in the same boat along with us.

We realized that the medical bills were our obligation but at this point we had no idea even what the total amount owed was and actually who we were indebted to. The list was massive and we knew some action had to be taken. We had completed reams of paperwork begging for financial assistance but because I had insurance through my very meager retirement, little help was available. Social Security Disability had refused my claim twice but I still reapplied again. I was advised to get an attorney and force Social Security to come through for me but it seemed that process was simply beyond our capability at this point. Our charge cards were maxed out and we could no longer make those payments. We were behind on our mortgage and every month it was a constant struggle to keep the utilities from being disconnected. We had even rolled every penny in the house just to buy groceries. Do you have any idea how embarrassing it is to take twenty-five dollars worth of pennies into a grocery store? We do.

We made an appointment to see a bankruptcy attorney. After explaining our precarious situation, he told us we really had no other choice available to us than filing for debt relief. He gave us a large packet containing all the requirements and our job was to provide a listing of everyone we owed money to. It was an arduous task. The assignment was overwhelming but finally I sat down ready to wade through the sea of financial ruin and file Thirteen-A.

For more than a year, we had simply filled that cardboard box. It took more than a week just to sort out the mess. Having an administrative background, I made a computer database that would list everyone of our creditors, account numbers and amounts owed. We were astonished at the bottom line figure which was well over a half million dollars. We submitted the paperwork to our bankruptcy attorney in November 2006. Finally, we would have some relief. It took another two weeks until all of our creditors were notified of our financial intentions and slowly the phone stopped ringing. Blessed silence, constant admonishment from harassing collection agents were over. We still had one persistent collector who refused to stop calling. This "attorney" or so she called herself, unleashed the most awful venom on us because of a hospital bill we couldn't pay. The bill totaled over ten thousand dollars. We'd explained our situation, tried to be reasonable, but the woman hurled insults and degraded us with ugly names. It amounted to verbal abuse and we simply began hanging up on her when she'd begin calling at six a.m. After we were finally able to turn her name and information over to our attorney, those calls stopped as well. The bankruptcy went to court in December 2006. Not one creditor showed up to dispute the case. With the dawning of 2007 our debt relief was finalized. We had managed to keep our house and vehicles, for that we were truly grateful.

An unexpected blow came by mail one fateful afternoon when the family doctor I'd been seeing for sometime now sent a form letter stating he would no longer see me. The letter was brief and reflected no personal feeling whatsoever. Because of my "refusal" to meet my financial obligations, the fact I had filed bankruptcy and left them holding a balance, left him unable to render any further medical services ... medicine is a business after all. The form letter was signed sincerely ... excuse me, sincerely. We felt the doctor probably had no idea the letter was sent. This was strictly a "business" decision. I felt as if it was just one more punch in the gut that seemed to keep coming at me.

I guess I should be accustomed to medical personnel coming in and out of my life by now. But starting over with a new doctor was tiresome and complicated. Unfortunately, now I was plagued with beginning with all new medical staffs except for my tried and true urologist—who has incidentally bent over backward trying to help me. He has gone as far as writing off portions of my balances because he knows how financially strapped we are. It does my heart good to know there are a few doctors still out there who put their patient's needs first.

After the exhaustive search to find a doctor willing to see me, I had a new "family doctor." She agreed only to treat me for the various simple complaints—just the average garden variety health issues. She would see me for no gastric problems and nothing too serious, though nothing is easy in my case. I felt comfortable in her care but like the other doctors, I still had no "extra" money to pay her the remaining balance after my medical insurance met its requirement. The office manager of this doctor's practice was an extremely rude and seemingly uncaring individual. She hounded me for money each and every time I called for an appointment or was in the office, which I was at least three or four times a month. Even though I couldn't afford it, I reluctantly agreed to pay twenty-five dollars a month (I know that doesn't sound like much but when that's your grocery budget for the week, it's more than I could handle), but in fact we didn't have that. We really weren't surprised when a little more than six months later a letter was delivered (certified even) that stated this doctor could no longer preside over my medical care as well. At least I would be spared from the torment of that awful office manager but again I felt abandoned. The fact was, I had developed an inability to trust in any medical provider. Eventually all of them would "hurt" you, if not physically then emotionally or by desertion. This was a dangerous mental place for someone in my position, but it was a learned response and a reality of my situation.

My morale was low and my health was declining. At this

point, we had no alternative but to return to the university hospital to unfamiliar doctors. Dealing with strangers when you're sick and afraid is very unnerving. I was at the mercy of whoever had a spare moment to treat me, the doctors changed daily. It was determined that because of my steadily decreasing weight and malabsorption problems, it was in my best interest to have the feeding tube replaced. Surgery again. I would get to see my pals in the surgical suite. Familiar medical staff! And they are all truly great people! The placement of the tube went through without a hitch and within an hour I was languishing in the recovery room. After a two hour observation period, I could go home. We were then advised I needed to have the feeding tube routinely changed every three to four months; hopefully this would preclude my body rejecting it again.

Suddenly, there in the recovery room, I began to shiver. My husband alerted the nurse that something was wrong. She checked my vital signs, which showed I had a steadily rising fever. Here we go again! They called a doctor immediately. Soon a surgical resident stood at my bedside. She prescribed Tylenol, then ordered that once my fever broke, I could be released. The nurses went ballistic and that is a huge understatement.

For the first time at the university hospital, we requested this surgical resident not be allowed to supervise any of my further treatment. I hope she will eventually learn to have a better bedside manner and ability to treat her patients with a caring persona or I fear another physician, much like the one who performed my original surgery, will soon be licensed to practice medicine on other unsuspecting patients (a very unsettling thought). My husband reported our feelings concerning this resident to the head of the university surgical department with hopes the concern would be addressed. However, we had other problems to deal with just now.

Hospital rules specifically stated that, "no one running a fever greater than one-hundred degrees after surgery can be released under any condition." The resident had concluded this was just a little post-op temperature and nothing at all to worry about. Wonder if she had ever read my chart? By then my fever had soared to one hundred four degrees. The recovery room nurses consulted a surgeon who happened to be walking through at that time. Lucky guy right? Though I was not his patient, on their recommendation, he examined me. Instantly, he determined I was in no condition to be released. He ordered up my usual suite in ICU. The surgeon ordered blood work to identify the bacteria causing this raging fever.

The tests revealed nothing out of the ordinary, yet the fever continued to plague me. Obviously, there was some sort of infection, but what? The doctor ordered every test under the sun, still no answers. Finally, multiple blood samples went to the CDC in Atlanta for identification, I had possibly become their biggest lab rat. The wait began... again. We were left wondering, what now? Again. The fever eventually abated after ten days and I was put on six weeks of antibiotics at home, in isolation again. It was determined that the MRSA had flared up again and that this would be something I would have to deal with the rest of my life. The doctor's determined that from this point forward I should never have surgery, at least not planned surgery, before undergoing at least two weeks of antibiotic therapy. Home again, home again, I was going home again!

A new worry was dawning on our narrowed horizon. After contemplating the decision for months, my youngest son timidly approached us about taking him to see a doctor about fifty miles to the south who specialized in gastric banding surgery. He was terrified because of all that I had experienced. He wasn't committing to it but was interested in how gastric banding surgery worked, compared to my disastrous gastric by-pass procedure. I'd explained over and over again to him that just because I went through these complications didn't mean he would but gastric by-pass just was not an option as far as he was concerned. Who could blame him?

Our baby boy was then twenty years old and the scale soared somewhere over four hundred pounds. I don't know exactly how high the numbers reached but that is an educated guess. We didn't know it yet but this doctor would change our lives in more ways than we had ever anticipated. The first step was a gastric banding seminar.

After placing a call to his office, we were scheduled for a seminar two weeks later. The whole family assembled to attend. When the evening arrived, of course, we were running late. The room was virtually filled to capacity with the only available seats at the very front row center so, of course, every eye followed us as we took our seats. You know what they say about first impressions? The man standing at the front of the room, who welcomed us as we walked through the door, was very handsome and had a voice you could listen to for hours. But we were soon to learn that outward appearances revealed nothing compared to the heart of this man.

Chapter Nineteen

~ NEW HORIZONS ~

T he seminar was complete with visual aids (even show and tell with an actual band demonstration), several patients who had undergone the gastric banding surgery spoke and a lot of other very valuable information released. I was really shocked at how simple the banding surgical procedure was compared to the much more serious and invasive gastric by-pass. Why hadn't I waited just a little longer for newer technology? Hind-sight is indeed twenty-twenty. Most patients who underwent the surgery were up and feeling great two or three days after the procedure and many had returned to work within forty-eight hours. When you think of the six weeks of down time with an open gastric by-pass, if things go well (and that is a big IF), the surgeries are like comparing apples and oranges. The banding does not alter your anatomical structure in anyway and the band can be very easily removed if necessary. The band removal is statistically warranted in less than three percent of the patients who undergo the procedure.

Then surprisingly the doctor asked had anyone present had a gastric by-pass. Reluctantly, I raised my hand. When asked, I briefly gave an accounting of my experience to this point and felt really guilty about doing so. I was quick to explain I had never met this doctor and was not an "audience plant." I proved his point dramatically concerning how dangerous gastric by-pass surgery can be.

I was extremely uncomfortable at the seminar in the

midst of these people who were begging for hope and relief in their battle with obesity. The one thing I didn't want was for the focus to shift to me as it always seems to do when other people begin hearing about all the troubles I've had. I didn't want any attention, least of all because of my numerous health issues. I'd rather be noticed for something else—how much I love my family and friends, my writing, my books, my home-town … anything … just not as an anti-gastric by-pass poster child.

My experience was certainly not meant to scare anyone away from gastric by-pass surgery. I have no intention of ever doing that. I simply want people to consider very carefully their decision and all of their options. The most important is-sue is to know the doctor well. This point is so important. I'll chant this mantra again and again. Know the surgeon. Know the surgeon. Become an authority on his practice and talk to everyone of his patients that you can. Go to the hospital and talk to the nurses, talk to his staff, ask questions about his or her reputation (both good and bad). Listen carefully to what the staff has to say about the surgeon. Check out his staff turn-over. If he changes nurses like changing underwear, stay away. If the doctor has trouble with his hand-picked staff, imagine what the treatment of patients with a variety of differ-ing personalities might be like.

Regardless, as the evening moved to a close the doctor had an emergency and was forced to leave rather quickly. Strangely enough, he was, by profession, a pediatric surgeon who does the gastric banding as well. That statement makes it seem like the banding is an afterthought, though that is far from the truth. He is very passionate about helping the masses suffering from obesity. He'd left the seminar to deal with an emergency concerning one of his pediatric patients. I found it rather strange that he works with the largest and the tiniest of patients. But when this doctor was caring for his patients, it's an amazing experience to witness. Further, the ease in which he combines the two specialties was a sight to behold. Because of the various differing complications, I've been grateful for his expertise in each profession.

After the seminar, I approached his nurse and asked if he

might be willing to see a gastric by-pass patient with some fairly serious complications. She agreed to ask the doctor and get back to me via email. I felt hope for the first time in a very long time. I crossed my fingers and said a silent prayer. I was impressed by his passion, knowledge, patient manner and expertise—pretty much in that order. I wanted an appointment.

I was surprised when I received a reply in very short order. My wait had only lasted about forty-eight hours when one of the most beautiful voices I've ever heard phoned to say the doctor would see me the following Monday … only four days away. Hope flooded my senses, I could barely sleep.

My health was not on one of the downward spirals at the moment but I wasn't feeling well either. I looked like death warmed over, but appearances can be a little deceiving. I had certainly been much worse. I was nervous about the upcoming visit. One just never knows and there were so many possibilities at play here.

Would the doctor scorn me for having the gastric by-pass at all? He didn't seem the type to berate his patients. Would he simply dismiss me as having "mental problems" as it had been in the past? I'd been down that road before and would never let anyone subject me to that kind of verbal abuse again. Never again—not ever. Would he offer nothing in the way of real help? All of these situations were possibilities and in fact, circumstances I'd found myself in before. Anticipation can be the worst problem of them all.

Many of my previous doctors have been content with just treating my symptoms and resolving no health issues at all. I wanted some resolutions. I wanted my life back, at least some semblance of a life. I wanted to be able to do the simple things in my life that meant a lot to me. It just didn't feel like too much to ask to have a half-way "normal" life. I would have been happy with simply not going to the hospital twice a month, or once a month for weeks at a time. I've seen too many hospital rooms, too many emergency rooms and too many medical personnel.

The few days seemed to pass at a snail's pace. I was impatient, nervous, the suspense was wearing me thin. I searched for anything to keep my mind from imagining what was to come when I finally met the new doctor. Unfortunately, my imagination was working overtime. The various scenarios flashed through my brain like continuous play videos. Please Lord, get me through this, I prayed. I had been down this path too many times and the results could be disastrous or great. Only God knew what was in store for me and he wasn't sharing at this point.

The morning of the appointment finally arrived. My beloved husband had looked up the directions and knew where we going. He had made a copy of my huge medical file, at least what we had of it. The stack of paper weighed (no joke) over five pounds. I had a listing of all my medications and had written out a list of my chief complaints, highlighting those that tended to be the most chronic. We were armed for bear and ready to go.

When we arrived, negotiating the ridiculous parking lot was a dreadful challenge. The office itself is very nondescript and filled with toys for kids waiting to see the doctor. I checked in and took a seat in the crowded room while my husband stood outside away from the crowd. With the room filled nearly to capacity, mentally I prepared for a long wait and regretted not bringing a book to occupy myself.

Patients were chatting and everyone seemed strangely upbeat. The topic of conversation was, what else? Food. It's funny even when you can consume very little, people struggling with weight, regardless of what stage they're in, must discuss food. I believe it is some unwritten commandment. What do you eat? How much? When? What restaurants serve post-surgery friendly meals? Which ones are willing to discount your meal because you eat three bites and you're done?

I felt somewhat outside the club. I guess just having undergone gastric by-pass rather than banding, I didn't belong. I was out of their loop. Of course, my story would leave them feeling extremely grateful for their decision to have the banding rather than the more radical surgery. I didn't share my ordeal with any of them. It's funny to feel ostracized in this world, yet the whole thing was probably a segregation of my own doing. I felt guilty for having had the gastric by-pass to begin with.

The waiting room sit-in was not nearly as long as I thought it was going to be. In fact, I was quite surprise when after only fifteen minutes my name was called. I retrieved my husband and followed the nurse into the inner sanctum. Behind the secret doors (until you've broken the barrier, it seems to be some mystic place) didn't seem to be any different from the waiting room, nondescript. This was a very busy physician's office and little expense was spared for decoration. I felt somehow comforted in this. Perhaps the doctor cared more for his patients than a polished impression. At least, that's the way I interpreted the look of this place.

First stop, the dreaded scales. But these weren't just any scales. They were high-tech, Wham-o-dyne scales that would tell everything about you except maybe your shoe size. No, well maybe that darn thing knew that, too.

It was pure loathing upon first sight on my part for this tattle-tale device. No matter how thin or substantial one is, the scale is traumatic for nearly everyone. There were no blinking numbers on display. No this was much worse than that. The scale issued a print out so every little flaw was recorded in black and white! The only thing worse would have been a color-coded record identifying problem areas. Body fat percentage, water retention, body mass index, height, and oh yeah, weight! Probably the top five things, I really didn't care to know. The numbers always lead to a lecture. Of course, the only thing I had no control over was my height and I know I'm short.

The nurse took the usual vital signs and jotted down notes of my complaints. I had already forwarded my medical records, though I was not sure anyone had taken the time to wade through that mass of medical confusion. Still, it was my first visit and the folder bearing my name was pretty thick. Then the nurse stepped out and we were left to wait again.

Sequestered in the doctor's exam room, after you've read all the posters, you're left to your own devices. Most of us want to plunder through the cabinets and drawers just to see what's there. Alas, few of us actually follow through with the impulse but it is tempting. I sat in the hard plastic chair, ankles crossed, hands folded neatly in my lap for all of three minutes.

Then I was up and pacing the room. First, a close up view of the posters. Okay, that's finished, what next? I stepped off the length and width of the room, maybe ten-by-ten. The doctor better get here soon, I decided, I think I'm losing it. Losing what? Who knows?

I timed our wait with my Mickey Mouse watch. Five minutes, six, seven, eight … there was a knock on the door and in walked the tall, handsome man who was to become my new doctor. Now I was really nervous. He introduced himself and began to discus my condition. It became obvious he'd studied my chart and had formed a plan of action. We were shocked at that point. No doctor, not even my beloved university surgeon, had ever impressed us so much in one visit.

His plan of action involved my going to the hospital. Surprise, surprise, surprise. According to the doctor, I needed fluids and vitamins right away and he wanted to conduct some tests to find out just exactly what was and wasn't there anatomically. He wanted another feeding tube in place and to begin a regimen of protein supplements several times a day. I begged for the chance to go home, collect my things and take care of a little personal business. I really had nothing to take care of at home, I just wanted to go home and pack my own stuff. I think the doctor understood my position. He had the nurse schedule my hospital admission for Monday, five days away. I was somewhat relieved but not altogether joyful.

On Thursday, I began to feel pretty bad. By that evening, I was vomiting. By Friday morning, it was obvious I needed medical care. We had a choice—either our local emergency room or calling on my new doctor. We knew a trip to the emergency room would take hours and I'd probably get little, if any, relief. I called my new "baby doc" and only managed to get through to his service. Hope dwindled for me.

Within ten minutes, our phone was ringing and the doctor advised my immediate admission into the hospital. He told us orders would be waiting when we arrived and to get there as soon as possible. This wasn't an optional thing now. I packed my bag, prepared for a week stay and off we went. I retched into a hospital pan the entire route and by the time we arrived, I was physically and emotionally spent. I simply needed some relief from the nausea and pain.

The waiting began. We've found that communication is never good between the hospital and doctors offices. We arrived and walked into hospital admissions and they had no idea who I was or why I was there. Of course, the story is always the same. We sat while supposedly the admission clerk was checking on the situation and trying to find my orders. She was ineffective. I was totally embarrassed by my lack of control as I vomited in the basin and other patients did their best to avoid the sight of me. Been there. Done that. It was a very unpleasant situation.

Finally after a forty-five minute wait, we saw my doctor sprinting across the lobby and heading for the front doors. I weakly called his name and his attention fell to me sitting pitifully in the waiting room. He and his patient representative had been searching the entire hospital for me. I was supposed to be tucked into a bed with medication to ease my suffering at this point. He was livid concerning the delay. He was immediately on his cell phone making things happen. A wheel chair and syringe arrived at the same time. There in the lobby he gave me medication, sending me off to a room to be settled in and saying he'd see me a little later on and let us in on the game plan. Relief finally began to numb my tortured body and I let the oblivion wash over me. I don't remember being tucked into bed at all.

A knock on the door roused me from a murky depth and I noticed that it was dark outside. Hours had obviously passed as my handsome doctor walked through the door with a concerned look on his face. Preliminary blood work was not good (what's new about that?) and he intended to take steps immediately to rectify the situation. As soon as I was comfortable enough, the testing would begin. Search for a certain feeding tube which he preferred was already in progress. A specific size had to be found and it was not readily available.

Finding the feeding tube became a long and arduous journey. It was called a Mickey Button. This particular feeding tube didn't extend from the body so it was less likely to be snatched out when changing clothes. Imagine something sewn into your body being ripped from a tender hole (I guess incision would be the more polite vernacular) in your abdomen quite suddenly. Believe me, it's not a pleasant experience. It happened often and if you tried to tape the tube in place to keep it out of the way then it would get crimped and that was painful as well.

The Mickey Button was not necessarily meant for adult patients, but I was small enough that it would be a perfect fit for me. Unfortunately, physically I wasn't in the greatest shape for surgery at the moment. My blood pressure was too low and I was severely anemic, sinking into a deep depression. More than anything I wanted to be well enough to be at home with my family for the holidays. I'm not sure why I always seem to fall apart during the fall and winter. One of my best buds says it's the weather but I'm not really convinced of that, yet I don't know that I can discount the theory either.

Over the course of the next few days endless tests were administered. Nothing too awful yet it wasn't a pleasant experience. The doctor came in one morning to let us know he really needed to "go in" and look around. "Go in", no matter how simply put is invasive and usually involves pain. We were anxious but consented. The results were very telling and quite surprising.

Once the procedure was over, the doctor knew for sure what we were dealing with and felt certain he could help me to some extent. He found I no longer had any stomach in the digestive tract. My esophagus was connected straight through to the intestine so my food had no where to breakdown. Because so much of my intestine had been removed, I no longer benefited from the vitamins and nutrients usually gained from food intake. The situation was irreversible and though I could live with the condition, I'd never have a "normal" life. On the brighter side, I didn't have to have a miserable life either.

The doctor felt my current health situation was unacceptable. I should be able to live free of pain. Though it sounds simplistic, the only thing we could hope for was a better quality of life. Other than treating the numerous complications as they occur, the only actual treatment was to change my current eating habits, which were atrocious, and to take in as much protein as possible. I'd gone through gastric by-pass to lose weight with hopes that dieting would be a thing of the past, now I find myself on a strict diet I'd have to adhere to for the remainder of my life. Obviously, dieting was, and is, a tough thing for me. I'd never been successful before, hence weight-loss surgery. It seems now I've come full circle.

After finally being released from the hospital, I received a letter from social security announcing my disability had finally been approved. Relief flooded over me. I felt as if the tide were turning in my favor. This was a new concept I readily accepted.

Chapter Twenty

~ FOR TODAY ~

The struggle continued day-by-day, which is better than hour-by-hour. The big question always asked of me was, "Would I do it all over again?" The answer is complicated.

My standard response and what I truly believe, vanity is not worth my life. I like being thin but what I have been through the past six years and continue to live with everyday of my life, leads me to believe I wouldn't go through the surgery again. Remember the saying "if I knew then, what I know now?" As they say hindsight is twenty-twenty but if I could go back into the past and select a different initial surgeon, then I might do it again. I believe in this surgery when it is done correctly. The surgery can drastically change and, in fact, save the lives of obese people. Pre-op testing should be stricter to weed out those who have a high risk of dying as a result of the surgery. Unfortunately, those are the very people who have the highest risk of dying as a result of obesity complications.

Selecting your doctor is definitely the most important factor in the decision to gastric by-pass surgery. I realize I drive that point into the ground, but very seriously, no part of the process is more important. It's imperative that you select the best surgeon for the job or quite honestly (according to research), you raise the risk of death by fifty percent. Even though I did two years of extensive research, found out as much as possible about my surgeon, I ended up with an incredible jerk who had no business "practicing" medicine.

I spoke with many of his patients as well as checking on any complaints through the American Medical Association. I simply chose the wrong man to operate on me. After my first interview with him, I had some reservations because he failed to answer a number of my questions. His attitude was brisk and short as if he had somewhere else he'd rather be and it seemed I was taking up too much of his time. The doctor had no aftercare program at that time. He had no dietician on staff and seemed much more concerned with how I would pay the balance over and above what my insurance would cover. Money seemed to be his major motivation. In fact, the doctor only agreed to meet with me briefly until the insurance approved the surgery.

The basic lesson I've learned has been to pay more attention to my gut instincts. I had the opportunity several times to walk away from this doctor but I was blinded by hope. The promise of weight-loss was far too enticing. I felt as if his substandard care and hateful bedside manner was all I deserved. I'm worthy and I have to continue to remind myself of that fact.

No matter what your appearance or your economic status may be, no one deserves sub-standard medical treatment. I'll repeat it again for those who continue to feel inferior (most obese people do). No one deserves sub-standard medical treatment. Talk about equal rights, obesity is a classic example.

When the surgeon recorded my weight, I lacked seventeen pounds meeting the one hundred pounds overweight criteria for insurance approval. The surgeon's advice was to eat as much as possible to gain twenty-five pounds. He misled my insurance provider by padding my weight figures. He aggressively tried to convince me to have the surgery laparoscopically because he had only recently observed the dynamics of how to do the procedure and needed patients to consent to be his first "victims."

As I explained in the beginning, I refused repeatedly, it was the one point I refused to concede. Even after I expressed to him I didn't want to be a laparoscopic practice case, he offered me a monetary discount if I would agree. I stood my ground and said no. I was nervous that he'd done a limited number of *roux-en-y* surgeries at that time (today, it is my understanding that his practice does around thirty a month). Desperation makes a great catalyst. He treated me like just another payday. Once he saw my folder containing all of my research on the surgery, the surgeon told me I already knew everything I needed to know about the surgery and there was nothing else he could tell me. I simply needed to make my decision and he was finished with me.

Feeling guilt over my decision is a burden I'll always carry. I put responsibility squarely on my own shoulders. I should've listened to my instincts and sought out another doctor. However, because of my extremely low self-esteem, I subconsciously felt I didn't deserve any better treatment. I have never admitted to this abject opinion of myself to anyone, however, that was the way I felt. Please, if you get nothing else from this book, understand each and every one of us are worthy of the best our medical professionals have to offer. I hid behind a confident façade for those around me. In my heart, I didn't believe I was entitled to respect, courtesy or kindness from this or any other healthcare provider. I was willing to place my life in his hands. I did put my life in his hands, yet I recognized him as a callous, despicable human being. The ironic thing about my self-image is that I don't project that opinion on others.

For example, I believe my beautiful sister deserves the best of everything and should anyone dare treat her with disrespect or come up short in their care of her, I would be livid. I would not, under any circumstance, tolerate the very same behavior I was exposed to for anyone I love. I'd go to bat against any offender without a second thought. Why don't I value me as much?

My health today is like flipping a coin. We never know from one moment to the next how I'll be feeling. One simple thing can throw me over the edge and the vomiting, diarrhea and pain can be instantaneous. I might eat too fast, too much or my body just rejects what I've eaten for no apparent reason and I'm in sudden distress. If my sinuses are draining or I'm passing the weekly kidney stones, the vomiting and unrelenting pain is back. As of this moment, I'm doing pretty well.

I've been a little more active lately and in response, I began to lose weight. I can't afford to do that. The doctor has told me if at any time I'm considered malnourished, I'll have to return to the hospital and the magic number is less than one hundred fifteen pounds.

The surgery alters the physical body but the mind of an obese person is still there. I see myself as obese even at one hundred twenty pounds. When the scale numbers creep up, even as little as three pounds, I begin to panic. The fat girl is coming back. It is nothing more than water weight but still the thought of going through the agony of obesity remains. At the time of this writing, it has been three months since my last hospital stay. This is the longest stretch spent without a hospital admission in the past six years. After more than sixty hospital stays, more emergency room visits than we can remember, six feeding tubes, abundant scars and flabby skin, I'm still here. I'm still alive. I still pray daily that the decision to submit to gastric by-pass surgery won't cost me my life.

My life since gastric by-pass surgery has not been all bad. It's that statement which allows me to continue to support the procedure when done correctly and with the right motivation. The surgery won't solve all of your problems, it'll make some of them worse … but it can do wonders for your self-esteem and the person looking back at you from the mirror each morning. I like her again.

I've never felt such a thrill as one afternoon in a local department store when I tried on blue jeans. I tried a size twelve—too big, size ten—too big. Then I held a pair of size nine jeans in my hand, slipped them on and buttoned them up without having to suck it in (you know what I mean). The nines were a little loose. Could I possibly try on an eight? No way! I did, they fit like a glove. I've not worn clothes in single digits since I was in elementary school. I was elated. I bought a pair in every color and couldn't wait to get home to show them off to my husband. I even did deep knee bends to make sure I could still breathe with them on. I could!

I felt more confident, pretty and why not? I'm a very worthy person deserving the accolades of all my hard work. My sister and I recently went on a girl's day out together to a well-known theme park. All of her adult life, she's been too large to ride most of the attractions. We love roller coasters. We rode them all that weekend, some of them several times. Not once did we need a seat belt extender or were embarrassed because the restraints wouldn't fit. We fit and we had fun!

I keep an old picture of myself in my purse. I love to show it to people and see the shock on their faces concerning how much weight I've lost. Wow, if they only understood how difficult the process had been they'd be astounded. But I look nice now and that was my ultimate goal. I did expect to keep my health, but I guess that's the price I'm paying for being thin.

This surgery can change your life for the better if you have a surgeon who cares. By that I mean, a doctor who really cares about his patients and puts their needs before the insurance payment. I pray that perhaps by reading this some gastric by-pass patient realizes there are complications. They don't happen to everyone but the possibility is there. Don't ever let your doctor get away with treating you like a number or another notch on his scalpel. If that doctor isn't the right one for you, walk away, there are many other doctors out there. This is your life. Don't let heartfelt desires overwhelm your good sense like I did. Don't ever let anyone make you feel inferior. You're paying the doctor to serve you.

Recently, I went to my twenty-fifth high school reunion. I walked into the place like I owned the joint. I looked better than I've ever looked as an adult and people who would never have spoken to me back then made it a point to seek me out that night. I felt like the queen of the ball, but it was because of what was inside me, not anything anyone else could project on me. Gastric by-pass surgery has given me self esteem, I like the way I look (except during the bad days when I look like death warmed over), but for the most part, my goal has been achieved, I am thin.

Chapter Twenty-One

~ *THE PRICE OF BEING THIN* ~

So what is the price of being thin? For me, it has been very much like making a pact with the devil. In other words, be careful what you ask for, you just may get it. The price has been extremely high, more so than I could have ever anticipated or imagined when I was considering the surgery. The Mayo Clinic has issued a statement that says one in every five gastric by-pass patients have marginal to excessive complications. Twenty out of every one thousand patients die within the first thirty days after surgery and seventy-five die within the first year. Those are not very good odds. The surgery has cost me my health, my freedom, my career, strained my relationship with my husband (because we've lost intimacy and to a great extent our physical relationship), ruined our family financially and left my emotions in a mental uproar.

The major price has been the pain this experience has cost me. The physical pain is often more than I can stand. I will find myself knotted into a fetal ball trying unsuccessfully to relax as gas pains rack my body. The bubbles grip my intestine with an iron fist, then I feel some unexplained rumbling course through my innards, lengthening the spasm as it moves. The sharp pains clutch my chest and I panic in fear of a fatal heart attack. Kidney stones are very common complications in gastric by-pass patients, yet that isn't something most physicians mention. Urinary tract infections are frequent, especially when the sharp spines of stones tear through the tender flesh and shred the urinary tract. How long can my kidneys take this abuse before they're permanently damaged? No doctor can answer that question for me. Recently, a study was released stating that those with diminished kidney capacity (i.e. dehydration, frequent infections and kidney stone production) are sixty percent more likely to be diagnosed with renal cancer. It worries me that all the abuse to my kidneys will eventually weaken them until they fail and I'll be on permanent dialysis.

All gastric by-pass patients have, to some extent, vomiting called dumping syndrome. At first nausea gives the first warning of what's to come. More times than not the feeling gives way to dry heaves as though my very soul is straining to be forced from my body. My eyes bulge with the exertion of the throe. My ribs ache from the torture. I am left totally spent, my energy depleted, leaving me weak as a new born baby.

Then there are the horrible sudden spasms of diarrhea. I'm left drained and depleted, my entire system dehydrated and exhausted. Alternately, if I should try to quell the diarrhea I become impacted. Impaction feels as though my entire body will split apart with the shear pressure of the obstruction. Even pain medication will from time to time, leave me unable to go to the bathroom, giving me excruciating cramps and severe pain.

Often I am given strong drugs to help contend with the constant pain. Then because I take a huge amount of medicines for differing symptoms, sometimes these things will cause me to experience either drug withdrawals or interactions. The condition often leaves my legs twitching and my feet feeling as though the soles were on fire. A nervous feeling courses through my body with an inability to control my crawling flesh.

I have developed insomnia. In order to get a good night's sleep I must depend on a sleeping pill or remain awake all night. Without them, I'm awake for days on end, which brings on considerable anxiety. Often, the pills will leave me with memory lapses, which impairs my life to an extent, but what is the alternative?

Quite possibly, the hardest pain to deal with is the mental anxiety forced upon me through the helpless feelings of physical pain, weakness, not having enough strength to tend to my basic needs such as a simple shower or brushing my hair and teeth. Then there's the mental anguish left by the initial surgeon in saying the symptoms I experienced are nothing more than psychosomatic.

This doctor did more damage to me mentally than I've ever experienced from his butchery in surgery. I've a very frightening sense of paranoia that shouldn't be part of my daily life. The pain I feel, the anxiety, the despair at my situation are all natural feelings I'm certainly entitled to. They're very real and as intense as anything I've ever endured. No one has the right to make light of my feelings, reactions and conditions. If only I could concentrate on that uplifting mantra when I'm feeling at my wits' end, but sometimes the overwhelming anxiety gets the better of me.

This surgery and the complications of it have cost me nearly six years of my life. I don't mean by just being bedridden, which I was, or in severe pain, which I have been, but I have no memory whatsoever of more than two years of my life. The time is lost to me. A time I can never get back that lost years of my life. The time lost with my husband, children, family and friends, saddens me greatly. I was very nearly comatose during this time, blinded by shear pain, dulled by strong medications and drowning in oblivion of desperation.

Imagine something as simple as going into a restaurant, once my first question would be a curiosity of how good the food would be, now I question if there is anything on the menu I can eat. Something I may be able to eat today, doesn't mean tomorrow I'll have the same results. One bite, one single nibble more than my altered system can accommodate doesn't leave me simply feeling full but the results are violent dumping. If I eat one bite too quickly behind another, all is lost and the meal is finished. I often try to make light of it saying, if I don't make it out of the restaurant with the food I shouldn't be charged. Many times a dinner plate is put before me and I realize today is not an eating day. Meat of any kind is nearly impossible and if I do manage to eat it, the food must be cut in tiny bits and be extremely tender. One bite of a green leafy vegetable or something high in fiber and gas pain grips my body, immediate vomiting and diarrhea is the sudden result.

Huge red welts frequently cover my legs, arms and torso, which have been diagnosed as my body taking protein from my connective tissues because of the lack of protein consumed. Simply put, it's my body feeding on itself for nutrients. I have two discs in my lower back that have deteriorated significantly resulting in osteoporosis much earlier than would be normal.

My teeth have literally fallen out, so the remaining top teeth had to be pulled and replaced with a denture. As I write this, I'm preparing to have the bottom teeth pulled as well. I'm terrified at the prospect of going through the process again. It was an excruciating experience before.

Once thick and luxurious, today my hair falls out by the fist full. In fact my entire body is going bald. I have gaping bald spots, leaving me extremely self-conscious. I feel embarrassed, even in the privacy of my own bedroom.

I am constantly dehydrated due to my inability to take in the necessary fluids. Therefore, at the whim of my insurance company, I get IV therapy through the visiting nurses. It seems the health insurance people take great pleasure in denying my claims and then going back and reinstating benefits. One week they will pay for the IV therapy and the next they won't. Their policies continually change and with all of the other issues we contend with, health insurance shouldn't be a source of concern but unfortunately it is. All of these problems can be directly traced to the malabsorption of nutrients from food and the lack of a proper diet.

I have a three times higher risk for hernias, ulcers, blood clots, infection and scar tissue stricture. Internal bleeding, severely low blood pressure, both hypoglycemia and diabetes are all significant problems we contend with everyday. All of these complications I have experienced over the past three years. Unfortunately, I have experienced every complication short of death. I live in fear that these problems have shortened my natural life span significantly. All that I can do is place my life in God's hands.

As a result of the surgery, I was forced into a medical retirement. The surgery cost me a career that I had spent nearly twenty years building. But in the end I had very little choice. I was unable to work a regular schedule due to the fact that I never knew when sudden incapacitating illness would strike and I'd be admitted to the hospital. Because of the loss of my job, and the fact that my husband has had to decline work to care for me over the past six years, our financial situation is dire. We have no savings, we have borrowed money from both our families and friends as well as maxing out every credit card we had in order to keep our home and even today, we remain under the threat of losing it. Our credit report shows an abundance of unpaid hospital, doctor and other medical bills totaling more than five hundred thousand dollars in addition to the over two million dollars that my health insurance provider has paid. Oddly enough, even as I write these figures, I can't imagine those amounts of money, a fraction of those amounts is beyond what I am able to fathom. Maybe one day…

The surgery doesn't change ones self-image. I still see myself as that obese girl I've always been. So what have I gained? I obsess over even a tiny weight gain of two or three pounds. My baby surgeon looked at me and said, "You're thin, you do realize that, don't you?" No, I don't. Large bags of skin hang underneath my arms, my thighs, my rear and my breasts, which were all enhanced by the fat I've lost. Plastic surgery to remove this excess skin is difficult, not covered under any insurance and is extremely expensive. In my case, no reputable plastic surgeon would touch me, even if I wanted the surgery, because my health is so unstable.

I experience a great deal of guilt because I elected to have this surgery so in essence I've done this to myself. I feel responsible for the worry I've put my dear family and friends through. We would never be virtually penniless and in deep trouble with our financial status had I not decided to have this surgery.

As was a definite problem in my case, the American Medical Association (AMA) warns patients against choosing a surgeon who has literally watched other surgeons for a couple of days and returned to do gastric by-pass surgery themselves with little or no hands-on experience. The complication rates with these surgeons tend to be considerably higher than better-trained and experienced surgeons. I'm living proof that this conclusion is true. The AMA believes this surgery has largely become a moneymaking procedure rather than a medical need and patients are suffering numerous complications, as well as resulting in a very high mortality rate. The surgery to reverse a *roux-en-y* gastric by-pass is much more difficult than the initial surgery and is only performed in life and death situations, then more times than not, the patient is left in worse condition than before. Many patients, including myself, are led to believe that should complications arise, the surgery can be reversed. Reversal is not a viable option for anyone.

Although it is something often taken for granted, I have lost my freedom. I'm no longer able to travel, even locally, alone. I must always have medication easily at hand and someone must always be with me because my condition can change in the blink of an eye. I have to either remain at home or travel with my IV pole and pumps so my weekly fluid infusions to waylay dehydration can be administered. My daily dosage of nutritional supplements is pumped into my feeding tube so I can maintain a reasonable weight.

I have concentrated on the negative side of this surgery because that has been my experience, however, there are benefits. Many patients see improvement in severe health concerns such as diabetes, high blood pressure, sleep apnea and acid reflux. Patients can expect to lose nearly seventy percent of their excess weight in a very rapid manner, usually within the first year. Obese people are forced, at least at first, to modify their diets. The ease of movement becomes simple when the excess bulk has been reduced and the patients' self esteem and confidence experience a marked improvement. The ability to fit into regular-sized clothing and shoes is a definite boost to the ego. Even the simplest things are taken for granted such as sitting in a restaurant booth or on a chair without fear of breaking it, not having to purchase two plane tickets in order to accommodate the excess bulk or have a seat belt extension.

So what has been the price of being thin for me? Well, I guess one could conclude that it has cost me life as I have always known it. All of the things people take for granted every day are real losses for me. Health, freedom, finances, career, eating normally without vomiting, the ability to do anything strenuous or do things I've always enjoyed such as swimming, scuba diving or gardening, time with my family and friends. These are all things I have lost to gastric by-pass surgery.

Individuals must gauge for themselves whether these risks are worth going through this surgery. I'll say it again … I'm not anti-weight loss surgery, even now with all I've been through. I only hope and pray that no one has to go through the shear hell I've experienced.

Be advised, visit several doctors and choose one you feel comfortable with. Don't just pick the first doctor your insurance company recommends, unless he's the right man for the job. The price of being thin through gastric by-pass surgery can be extremely high, consider it carefully.

Chapter Twenty-Two

~ IS THERE AN UPSIDE OF GASTRIC BY-PASS SURGERY?

Even with all the complications I've had since my initial surgery, there have been definite good things that have resulted. Yet, there is an obvious reason this is the shortest chapter in the book. The reason for having the surgery in the first place was to lose weight. I've lost nearly one hundred fifty pounds. Unfortunately, because the doctor did a severely aggressive surgery, much more than was necessary, I have trouble maintaining weight now but thanks to my "baby doctor," I usually weigh in the vicinity of one hundred thirty pounds. Incredibly, that is about fifteen pounds less than I intended but as long as I can maintain that number, I'm not considered underweight. Matter of fact, on some "insurance charts," I'm still considered over weight though not obese. Imagine the constant struggle, going from obese to underweight, to whatever it is I am today. I never imagined this journey … not in my wildest dreams.

When I began this trek, I wore a woman's size twenty-two, now I generally wear a size six or eight or ten... according to the clothes maker, the sizes vary greatly. I guess most women are aware that clothes sizes vary, I was oblivious.

After I had lost considerable weight, I was so excited, I bubbled to my husband, "I'm wearing clothes in single digits." He had no idea what I was talking about, clothes size meant nothing to him. Since then I've dropped to my current size, I've become a regular clothes hound (until recently when our local consignment store discontinued their dollar rack). I've always hated shopping for clothes but now I can wear so many fashionable beautiful things I've never been able to wear before. It was thrilling.

As I've stated before, for the majority of my life, I've suffered from very low self-esteem, because of my weight. Even though I can't say this was magically cured because I'm thin now, I do feel better about myself. The bluster I've always used to hide my insecurities is now a genuine outgoing nature. I'm much more comfortable in public speaking situations, publicizing my books. I find it much easier to approach people when doing research for my books or even facing the various booksellers promoting my work. No longer do I have to hide behind a false sense of bravado, I feel much more confident. I believe this comes from the fact that I don't feel everyone is judging me because of my weight. It's much easier to disregard what someone else might think of you when you feel good about yourself.

Mobility has become much easier for me. My knees, ankles and feet no longer ache with the stress of the extra weight after doing something as simple as grocery shopping. It doesn't take my breath away to bend to tie my shoes. Taking care of my personal hygiene needs is no longer a difficult chore. I don't worry when sitting on a chair that it might break with my weight. I can fit into a restaurant booth with ease and it's no longer painful to sit in a movie seat that was too small for my bottom. I'm not sure if it's an asset from surgery or a hindrance to my relationship with my husband but never before was my husband jealous when other men would take a second look at me. Of course, when I was obese, men didn't look a second time. Recently, we were at a party with a number of our sons' friends who we'd never met before. One of the young men whispered to my older son, "Who's the hot woman over there?" My son responded, somewhat offended, "Gross man, that's my mom." That's a story I'll cherish well into my old age!

I guess the greatest benefit is that I like myself now. That's a huge statement. I want to take better care of me. I pay more attention to my hair, nails, makeup and clothes because I want to put my best appearance out there for all to see. During the summer I frequented the tanning bed so that I'd look nice … sun-kissed in sleeveless wear and sundresses. Not that I didn't take care in my appearance before but I was always trying to minimize my body with certain clothing, hide a double chin with shaded makeup or do anything to draw less attention to myself. I still dress fairly conservative but that has more to do with my upbringing and what I feel is "appropriate" for a woman of my age. However, I've found myself being a little more daring with my choices.

The complications of surgery I've suffered have been immense but equally as important are the benefits I've achieved. Feeling good about oneself is perhaps the best attribute anyone can have. It influences every part of life and the way one acts. I know the boost in my self-confidence has meant the world to me. The ego enhancement has helped me to maintain a steadfast attitude that I can and will survive this. I am worthy, a worthwhile human being. I deserve and you deserve the best that life has to offer.

Is there an upside to weight-loss surgery? Yes, there is and I've no doubt benefited. Was it worth all the pain? I don't think so.

Chapter Twenty-Three

~ OTHER VIEWS ~

My sister had what could loosely be referred to as "successful" surgery. Successful in that she's had very few complications but things were not exactly rosy for her either. She's been tormented by excruciating gas pains and one bite too much or eating too fast results in unproductive dry heaves.

She's become extremely frustrated, mainly due to the fact she'd been unable to lose as much weight as she would've liked. In fact, she's able to eat most anything in much larger quantities than she was initially capable of, which indicates she'd managed to stretch her gastric pouch. It's possible she could regain a drastic portion of the weight she has suffered to lose. Still, there are foods that cause her to dump instantly, particularly things loaded with sugar. She has also suffered with kidney stones and urinary tract infections. Tests have shown that she has the first indicators of early onset osteoporosis from calcium malabsorption. Recently, a bone scan revealed that her osteoporosis is much further advanced especially for someone of her age. She has the bones of a sixty year old woman at nearly half that age. Protein deficiency has caused her to have considerable hair loss with every washing. Like me, she will have to take nutritional supplements for the remainder of her life. Remember, this was a "successful" surgery. Does my sister regret her decision to have gastric bypass surgery? I don't think so.

There have also been numerous positive results of my sister's gastric by-pass. Amazingly, she has lost over one hundred fifty pounds, high blood pressure is no longer a grave concern and terrible bouts with acid reflux have been relieved a great deal. Her health is better than it's been in years. She's able to keep up with two active young boys as much as any mother is able to, and deal with the day-to-day rigors of her teaching position. Recently, she completed her Doctorate Degree in Education. She is an amazing, beautiful woman, both in appearance and where it matters most, she has an amazing heart. If it's not evident, I am extremely proud of her.

My brother-in-law is a wonderful man, a loving husband and father who has supported his wife through the entire process of gastric by-pass surgery and all that it entails. No one knows better than I do, (except for my husband and other spouses who have gone through this process) how difficult the spouse's position can be and how important that support is. He understands the struggle his wife has endured with her weight because he faces the same issues. He has cared for my sister through her recovery and knows first hand what effect the surgery has on your body. In addition, he has been privy to a great deal of the agony I've been through as well as the fact I've been close to death on more than one occasion. Taking all of it into consideration, my brother-in-law made the decision to undergo gastric by-pass surgery himself.

Once the decision to pursue the surgery was settled, he made an appointment with the very same surgeon who performed my sister's surgery. They were satisfied with her outcome and the care she'd received, so that was the easy part. He certainly met the criteria for the surgery. His weight exceeded the insurance requirement of one hundred pounds over what is considered his "ideal" weight. He has a rather serious situation with sleep apnea, diabetes as well as other co-morbidities or health conditions common in obese people.

Once the initial consultation with his selected surgeon confirmed he was indeed a candidate for the surgery, the next step was submitting the required paperwork to his insurance company. Those bells and whistles can be quite daunting but for the most experienced staff of his selected surgeon this process is a daily routine. Going into this process, they initially felt that since my sister had been approved by the same insurance company with relative ease, certainly her husband's process would prove no more difficult.

Time was of the essence. The company he worked for had been bought out and notified its employees that within the year they'd be closing the factory, which would be relocated to another state. My sister and her husband chose not to move with the company so at any time in the coming year, they could be told he no longer had a job. Therefore, if he intended to have the surgery, this was the time.

Several weeks after the insurance was filed, my brother-in-law received their decision. He had been denied. He went through a myriad of emotions from dejection to anger. In the end, he decided not to give up and filed an appeal. Unfortunately, that too was turned down. With a never say die attitude, my brother-in-law picked himself up and began trying again to lose the weight on his own. I wish him the best of everything and pray that whatever happens, he knows that we love him no matter what.

Recently, one of my doctors contacted me and asked if I'd be willing to speak with another patient who had gone through gastric by-pass using the same surgeon I had. I readily agreed when the doctor explained this couple had undergone the surgery together. The husband had no significant complications (at least not to date) but the wife suffered much like me. He wanted me to speak with the husband. I suggested that perhaps I should talk with the wife, rather than her spouse. The doctor further explained the wife, after having been dismissed by the maniacal surgeon with mental issues, had been unable to deal with the horrible complications. She committed suicide by putting a gun in her mouth and pulling the trigger. In my humble opinion, this surgeon is guilty of murder.

Finally, my youngest has consented to go through gastric banding surgery through my new doctor. Though he is extremely afraid due to my experience, something must be done to get his weight under control. At nearly five hundred pounds, the threat of death is very real. I trust this doctor with my son's life, which to me is much more valuable than my own. The thought of losing him is not something I can fathom.

I know many have survived the loss of a child but I can't imagine living without one of mine.

Today, my health is precarious at best. Repeated complications still plague me. In fact, I've just had surgery again as I write this to replace a failed port and anticipate an intestinal hernia surgery in the near future. Above it all, I'm alive. I take each day as it comes and deal with whatever it has to offer. I will not give up or give in to this awful condition. At least that's my stance for today, tomorrow I may have a different situation to deal with. It is my intent to press on, live my life to the fullest, whatever may come. What is the price of being thin? Still, I pray to God it isn't my life.

ABOUT THE AUTHOR

Valerie Evans Goddard has honed her writing skills over a span of more than twenty years. Her lifelong passion became lucrative when her author's voice found its natural tenor in her two most loved subjects, travel and history. She notes Eugenia Price, Flannery O'Connor, Margaret Mitchell and Lewis Grizzard as just a few of her favorites. She is currently working on her traveling series. Visit her website at authorsden.com /valerieevansgoddard.